**Paint
Your
Store**

Paint Your Store

How to Network Your Way to Your Next Career Move

(A Hiring Humans Book for Job Seekers)

Craig Fisher
(and Guest Writers)

Southlake, Texas

PAINT YOUR STORE

Copyright © 2025 by Craig Fisher

All rights reserved. No portion of this book may be reproduced or transmitted in any form or by any means, electronic or mechanical, including but not limited to photocopying, recording, or any information storage and retrieval system, without express, written permission from the publisher.

No part of this book may be used or reproduced in any manner for the purpose of training artificial intelligence (AI) technologies or systems, without express, written permission from the publisher.

Published by TalentNet LLC
401 N. Carroll Ave., Suite 202, Southlake, Texas 76092
TalentNetMedia.com
craig@talentnetlive.com

TalentNet LLC books are available at special quantity discounts for bulk purchase for sales promotions, events, fundraising, and educational needs. Special books or book excerpts also can be created to fit specific needs. For details and permission requests, write to the email address above.

Neither the publisher nor author is engaged in rendering professional advice or services to the individual reader. The ideas, procedures, and suggestions contained in this book should not be used as a substitute for the advice of competent legal counsel from an attorney admitted or authorized to practice in your jurisdiction. Neither the publisher nor author shall be liable or responsible for any loss or damage allegedly arising from any information or suggestion in this book.

ISBN 979-8-9889354-5-2 (eBook)
ISBN 979-8-9889354-4-5 (paperback)
ISBN 979-8-9889354-6-9 (hardback)

Printed in the United States of America

10 9 8 7 6 5 4 3 2

—

Copyediting by James Gallagher
Cover Art & Illustrations by Craig Fisher
Proofreading by Adeline Hull
Editing, Book Design & Publishing by Kory Kirby
SET IN MINION PRO

To my past self

Contents

Author's Note — ix
Introduction — xi

CHAPTER 1:
The Modern Job Hunt Has Evolved
(You're the CEO, and It's Full-Time) — 1

CHAPTER 2:
Know Yourself
(Career Clarity) — 9

CHAPTER 3:
Paint Your Store
(Build Your Personal Brand) — 19

CHAPTER 4:
Take the Leap!
(Use *The L.A.K.E. Approach*) — 31

CHAPTER 5:
The Content Blueprint—10 Lessons from a 700K-Follower Recruiter
(Featuring Guest Writer Joel Lalgee) — 43

CHAPTER 6:
Document Every Great Outcome
(Have Evidence) — 57

CHAPTER 7:
The Power of Networking, Referrals, and Stories
(Featuring Guest Writer Jim D'Amico) — **63**

CHAPTER 8:
Applying to Jobs
(The ATS Is Not Your Enemy) — **77**

CHAPTER 9:
Résumés That Recruiters Love—Inside Secrets for Landing Your Dream Role
(Featuring Guest Writer Trish Wyderka) — **85**

CHAPTER 10:
Impress, Don't Stress—A Human Approach to Job Interviews
(Featuring Guest Writer Erika Oliver) — **101**

CHAPTER 11:
Seal the Deal
(Start Strong) — **119**

CONCLUSION:
Be Human
(Always) — **127**

HEADS UP!
Beware of Job Scams
(Navigating the Hidden Dangers of the Job Search) — **133**

BONUS
Tools & Tech
(Take a Few Things With You) — **141**

About the Author — *151*

Author's Note

My first book, *Hiring Humans*, was predominantly written for the "hiring" perspective: attracting, converting, and retaining top talent in the age of automation. *Hiring Humans* explores how, yes, *we have cool tools*. Yes, *we have automation*. And, yes, *we should use these things*. But we can't forget that while we're using technology, we have to keep the human touch in human resources... *right?* Hiring is essentially a very human thing to do.

This book, *Paint Your Store*, draws on many of these same themes. There are even a few similar sections. The key difference is that *Paint Your Store* is written for the "job seeker" perspective: how to network your way to your next career move, customer, gig, business, or partnership.

Introduction

A few doors down from my house, in Grapevine, Texas, is a community park. In this park is a lightning-detector system. For those who don't live in North Texas, we sometimes get a lot of rain, thunder, and, of course, lightning. Yet there always seems to be a slight chance of sun—enough of a chance to go out for a walk, play in the park, or perhaps take a dip in a pool. Well, particularly in the summer, the detector goes off a lot, and it sounds like a tornado siren:

> *"Warning. Lightning has been detected.*
> *Get out of the park. Seek cover."*

People run away from the park. They get in their cars and run past my house with their dogs and their kids and their strollers. Until they hear . . .

*"All clear. You are clear to return. All clear.
You are clear to return."*

They get out of their cars and return to the park. People begin to walk past my house again, with their dogs and their kids and their strollers. Then, about twenty or thirty minutes later, the whole thing starts over again . . .

*"Warning. Lightning has been detected.
Get out of the park. Seek cover."*

For the past couple of years, we've been going through this pattern in our country, in our economy. A new warning or disaster or other alert sets me off almost every hour, on the hour, and then, oh no, everything's fine for a few minutes, and then we go through it again.

I see that this is happening, and I see you. I'm big on empathy. I know you're under a lot of pressure. I know you're busy. I know the job market is in an *interesting* place. I know what it's like to apply for jobs and that the process is slow, confusing, and time-consuming. I know how discouraging it is to navigate through a clumsy process and then . . . hear nothing. *Ghosted.* Part of this is because of the proliferation in technology and automation. Some would even say that AI is to blame.

I know you've said no to friends, family, travel, and fun for your job hunt. I know that finding a job *is a full-time job*. It takes a tremendous amount of time. You've probably submitted tens, if not hundreds, of résumés without getting any interviews. So you went back and changed your résumé. You hired and worked with a résumé writer. You paid someone to make sure it was applicant tracking system (ATS) compliant. But you still didn't get interviews!

Here's what I recommend:

Forget your résumé and forget applying to jobs. Instead, *paint your store.*

And the first step to painting your store is accepting that you are a personal brand. Whether you like it or not, potential employers "view" and "perceive" you, and the manner in which they do this is your personal brand.

Imagine your personal brand as a storefront, a vibrant display that tells the world who you are, what you offer, and why they should step inside. Just like a store, your brand needs to be inviting, memorable, and reflective of your unique strengths. It needs to showcase a compelling and authentic image that attracts the right opportunities and connections. Whether you're in the job market or looking to advance in your current role, painting your store with care and creativity is key to achieving lasting success.

If you're not getting interviews, changing your résumé in a million different ways won't help. What could be happening is that recruiters (and machines) are going to your online profiles, only to discover that there's not much going on. They see you haven't posted content and you haven't established yourself as the subject matter expert (SME) of the thing you want to do and be.

So kill two birds with one stone by creating and optimizing your online persona. Platforms like LinkedIn are great for this. Connect with the people who are doing the work that you want to do.

If you don't know what you want to do, you gotta figure that out (Chapter 2 is for you). Stop scattershooting and focus. Be the SME of you—*right?* Nobody knows what you can do better than you. And how's anyone else going to know if you don't actively share that thoughtfully, and intentionally, with the rest of the world on a regular basis?

So write interesting articles about the companies you want to work for. Share the articles online. Put them on LinkedIn and tag the people you have connected with. Show off what you can do.

Network your way to your next career move.

In this book I'm going to show you how. I'll cover some of my favorite strategies, ones that have helped me make money and stay employed doing what I want to do for the past thirty years.

I'll give you a quick example.

I Am a Professional Job Seeker

As a talent-attraction specialist, I help employers understand their candidate experience. I leak test candidate experience for employers. Meaning that *I apply to jobs for a living.* I place myself directly in job seekers' shoes and experience firsthand what it feels like to go through their hiring process.

I explore the following:

- How long does it take to apply?
- What is the communication from the employer like?
- How long does it take before you actually speak to a person?
- How does the messaging feel?
- What does the entire experience do to my (your) enthusiasm about the organization?

While a lot of these are hard measurables, some are soft statistics and key performance indicators (KPIs) that can and should be considered by employers. But the point is that I apply to jobs all the time. Every day I apply to jobs, and I send these employers a little report.

> *"Hey, I noticed this. If you ever want to talk about it, let me know."*

This is just me doing business development. And sometimes I will compare and contrast three or four employers that I've researched and applied to. I'll put a case study up online and tag all those employers in my post on LinkedIn. I might even make a video about it. And occasionally one of those employers will call me up and say:

> *"Hey, you know, we actually need some help with that."*

I'm sharing content. I'm being the SME of what I want to do for a living, *right?*

What You'll Learn

In the pages that follow, we'll explore these takeaways:

1. **Embrace empathy.** Understand the job-search process from both sides. Empathy for recruiters and hiring managers will help you stand out in the market.
2. **Be the SME of you.** No one knows your value better than you. It's your job to show the world what you bring to the table by being intentional about your personal brand online.
3. **Find your career sweet spot.** Uncover what makes you unique with activities like *The Focus List Exercise* to align your skills, passions, and market demand. This clarity will shape your job search and long-term goals.
4. **Build a standout personal brand.** From optimizing your LinkedIn profile to creating a business page, master how to

treat your online presence as your storefront and showcase your expertise with creativity and professionalism.

5. **Navigate career transitions strategically.** Use *The L.A.K.E. Approach* to identify adjacent opportunities and strategically build relationships that lead you to your ideal role.
6. **Use inbound marketing for your career.** Share content that showcases your expertise. I'll show you how to make opportunities come to you rather than constantly chasing them.
7. **Leverage video for visibility.** Discover how video content can increase your reach on LinkedIn and other social channels, amplify your voice, and position you as a thought leader in your industry.
8. **Keep a record of your success.** Learn to document your achievements, feedback, and testimonials to create a portfolio of evidence that highlights your value during interviews or pitches.
9. **Network your way to success.** Networking isn't just a tactic—it's your golden ticket. Master how to build meaningful relationships and get referrals that open doors.
10. **Craft résumés that recruiters love.** Follow insider tips to tailor your résumé for both human and automated readers, focusing on results-driven metrics and avoiding common pitfalls.
11. **Ace interviews authentically.** Prepare for interviews with the right mix of research, authenticity, and thoughtful follow-up, turning every meeting into a lasting impression.
12. **Seal the deal with confidence.** Evaluate and negotiate offers thoughtfully, then start your new role strong by aligning goals with your manager and continuing to build your personal brand.

13. **Balance tech with human connection**. Automation and AI are useful, but people still want human relationships. I'll teach you how to use both effectively in your job search.

By the end of this book, you'll have the strategies and tools to take control of your career and build a brand that makes employers want to work with you.

Let's get started!

PS: The overarching strategy detailed in this book works for sales and customer acquisition. Simply attract an audience and have them pay you to help them with something they need help with.

CHAPTER 1:

The Modern Job Hunt Has Evolved

(You're the CEO, and It's Full-Time)

So . . . this is my family in 1974. Yeah. From left to right, that's my dad and our cat, me and our dog, my sister, my mother, and our gerbil. This has to be a picture from the famous Olan Mills, right? It should be in a time capsule! It's here because, well, we all evolve, right? We're striving to be the best version of ourselves on a regular basis. It doesn't matter how old you are or how young you're starting; your goal is to be the next best version of you.

I was pretty cool then. I mean, look at that striped shirt. But I'm slightly better now (only slightly better). The point is that I've evolved. And you better believe the world has evolved too.

That's where I want to start our journey . . . with you, accepting the fact that:

You Have a Job

I like how Philip Atkinson, in his book, *Bee Wise* puts it:

"To turn your research lens back on yourself is a difficult, scary, and intimidating process. But it's important: Your career is your responsibility, not the company's. And you need to be the CEO of your own career. There is no longer such a thing as a job for life in a big organization. . . . Therefore, don't take anything for granted, don't stay static, and don't assume the world's not changing."[1]

If you do not have a job, *congratulations!* With a simple mindset shift, you can realize that *you're the CEO of your career.* After all, you're the SME of you, aren't you?

You see, nowadays employment means different things to different people. A regular job is not necessarily a regular job. There's gig work, contracts, projects, and so on. Little bits and pieces of work can turn into big work, and that big work can turn into full-time work with massive projects.

For most people, it's a mindset shift. An embrace of evolution.

You always have a job. Even if you're between roles. Your professional identity is no longer defined by a single job title or one employer. Instead, it's tied to your skills, experiences, and reputation—the thing I call your personal brand. That's a game-changing shift. It puts the power in your hands and lets you focus on your overall career journey, not just the position you hold at any given moment.

Think about your career as a portfolio—a collection of experiences, achievements, and roles that showcase your value. Each role you take on is a piece of that bigger picture. And here's the kicker: It's not about waiting for an employer to define who you are. You define it.

Once you define it, you can get paid for it.

---

[1] Philip Atkinson, *Bee Wise: 12 Leadership Lessons from a Busy Beehive* (Switzerland: BuzzWorks Publishing, 2025), 65-66.

To define it, you need to take your career portfolio and put it under an umbrella of sorts. If you're unclear about what to call it, just name it something general to give it a bit of flexibility. You'll want to allow for a natural evolution. Over time you can adapt and name it something that represents your work, your expertise, and your journey. This creates a strong foundation that shows you're always moving forward, always growing, and always building your value. Own it, because that's your business.

Once you do, you'll make it legit, and you'll always have a job. (I take you through this step by step in Chapter 3.)

You see, there are always people who want help and are happy to pay. Three to four small projects under your "umbrella" quickly turn into a full-time job.

I'll give you an example of this going really, really well:

Suleika Jaouad imagined graduating from college and becoming a journalist. Instead, she was diagnosed with an aggressive form of leukemia and underwent treatment. She was twenty-three, bedridden, and unpublished. Still committed to being a journalist, she started a blog and began reporting from the front lines of cancer. She started to "write and to take it seriously and to treat it as a job. It felt really good to have a job to do other than just being a patient." She set and met deadlines. She published the work that she wanted to do. One day an editor from *The New York Times* called and asked whether she wanted to write an essay. She thanked her but said no. She knew her time was precious and not guaranteed. She told this editor that she actually wanted to "write a weekly column from the trenches of treatment without knowing how my story was going to end, and to really give ink to that experience of illness in youth." To Suleika's shock, the editor said yes to trying it for a couple of weeks.[2] This column—Life, Interrupted—won an Emmy Award, and if you search her name on *The New York Times,* eighty-eight results come up.

This is what the "paint your store" concept is all about. Be the SME of you and showcase that online. It doesn't matter whether it's your personal website/blog, newsletter, Substack, Medium, or LinkedIn. The point is this: Create your job, assign yourself projects, and take it seriously.

Be the SME of what you want to do.

Don't wait for an employer to assign you the work you want; simply start doing it! And publish it. Build your brand and treat your career like the evolving, dynamic journey it is.

But, Craig . . .

"I don't know what I want to do . . ."

I'll pick up on this in Chapter 3, as I suppose I should throw some of my two cents at that, huh?

---

[2] Tim Ferriss, "Suleika Jaouad on Invaluable Road Trips, the Importance of a To-Feel List, and Finding Artistic Homes (#516)," The Tim Ferriss Show, June 1, 2021, accessed February 24, 2025, https://tim.blog/2021/06/01/suleika-jaouad/.

KEY TAKEAWAYS

- **The modern job hunt has evolved, you're your own CEO, and it's a full-time job.** Be the SME of you. Take charge. Adapt and evolve, because lifelong jobs are a thing of the past. Gig work, contracts, part-time projects, and short-term projects are here to stay.
- **Your career is defined by the personal brand you build, not by a single employer or job title.** Treat your career as a portfolio of achievements under a unique identity that reflects your expertise and journey. By owning this, you maintain control and always have a job, even between roles.
- **Create and own your personal brand.** Build your career under an umbrella name or identity that represents your expertise and journey. This branding helps you stay relevant and project your value consistently.
- **Be proactive.** Focus on building and showcasing your expertise. Don't wait for an employer to give you the work you want—start doing the work you want. Use platforms like blogs, newsletters, LinkedIn, or personal websites to publish projects aligned with your goals.

CHAPTER 2:

Know Yourself

(Career Clarity)

Start here:

Who are you?

What do you do?

What's unique about you?

These are the foundational questions you need to ask yourself at the start of your job search. Without clarity here, you're operating without a compass. These aren't just philosophical questions; they are the basis of how you position yourself to potential employers. (Or customers. In my view, customers and employers both answer the question of "How do you get paid?") If you don't have solid answers to these questions, take a step back. I suggest spending time reflecting on them, because your answers will become the core of your personal brand and the foundation of your job-search strategy.

It can be helpful to ask friends, coworkers, and colleagues to describe you, what you do best, and your unique traits.

Now let's get practical.

An exercise that I always recommend to people who are feeling stuck in their job search is something I call *The Focus List Exercise*. It's simple but incredibly effective in helping you figure out where to put your energy and attention when looking for a new role. Here's how it works.

The Focus List Exercise

The focus list is broken down into three main parts, and each part brings you closer to homing in on the job that's right for you:

1. **What have you recently been paid to do?** Think about your most recent roles. List out the tasks, projects, or responsibilities you were actually compensated for. This might not be the work you enjoyed the most, but it's important to start here, because it grounds you in reality. Employers pay for skills and services, so this list is a good reminder of the things you've proved you can do well enough to get paid for.
2. **What have you been paid to do that you also enjoy?** Now, from the first list, identify the things you've been paid to do that you actually like doing. This is key because it helps you filter out the work that doesn't align with your personal interests or strengths. You want to find roles that bring you both satisfaction and income. For example, you might have been paid to manage projects, but if you enjoyed

the client interactions more than the administrative side, that's a valuable insight.

3. **What are you most likely to get paid to do that you also enjoy?** Finally, focus on what you enjoy that is still relevant and in demand today. What are the skills or tasks you've been paid to do recently that are also aligned with your strengths and the current job market? The sweet spot is where your passions overlap with what employers are looking for—and that's where you want to direct your job-search efforts.

This third list is where you need to spend most of your time and energy. It's easy to get caught up in applying for anything and everything, but if you take this focused approach, you'll be far more successful in finding a role that's not only a fit for your skills but also one that you're excited about.

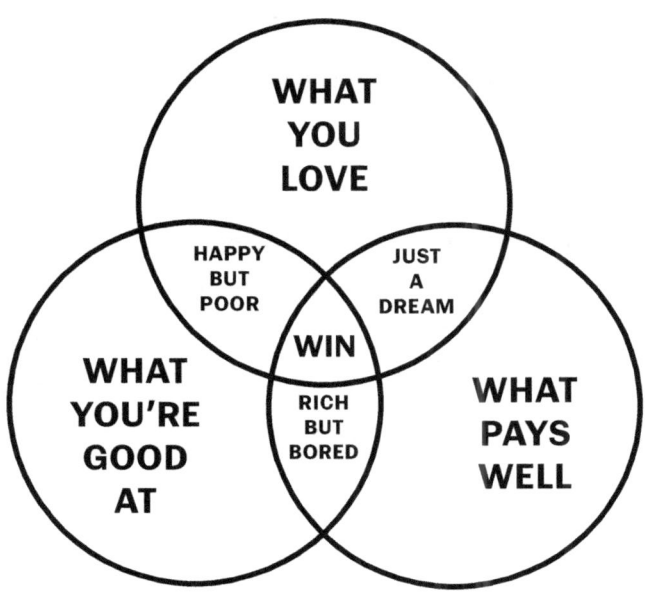

Narrowing Your Focus

Here's the truth: If you're willing to do *anything*, you're not focused enough. A common mistake I see is job seekers scattershooting—applying to anything that looks remotely close to their skills. They cast such a wide net that they end up with no bites at all. Employers can sense when you're not clear about what you want, and if you don't have focus, you won't stand out.

The purpose of this exercise is to help you stop scattershooting and narrow your focus. To help you home in on what you're good at, what you enjoy, and what the market values, giving yourself a clear direction. Once you've got this foundation, you'll be ready to build a targeted job search that positions you for the roles you're best suited for.

But this *Focus List Exercise* doesn't just help with job searching—it's a powerful tool for long-term career clarity. It'll guide you in making decisions on the projects you want, the roles you want to take on, the skills you want to develop, and the ways you want to build your personal brand and paint your store.

So take the time to know yourself, because the better you understand your own strengths and goals, the more effective you'll be in finding the right opportunities.

Get Started with Your Personal Focus List

There's no time like the present, so go ahead and try it out for yourself. You'll be amazed at how much clarity you can get by simply writing these things down.

1. What have you recently been paid to do?

2. What have you been paid to do that you also enjoy?

3. What are you most likely to get paid to do that you also enjoy?

Final Thoughts

In a world where your professional identity is no longer tied to one employer or one job title, it's critical to have this kind of clarity. Your career is a journey, and knowing who you are and what you do best is the first step to navigating it successfully. This exercise is a simple yet powerful way to get you moving in the right direction.

> **KEY TAKEAWAYS**
> - **Reflect on your identity and strengths.** Answer foundational questions: *Who are you? What do you do? What's unique about you?* Seek input from friends, coworkers, and colleagues to uncover your best traits and strengths.
> - **Try *The Focus List Exercise*.** Break down your professional experiences into three key areas:
>   - What you've been paid to do: List tasks and responsibilities from your recent roles.
>   - What you've been paid to do and enjoy: Narrow down tasks you find fulfilling and enjoyable.
>   - What you're likely to get paid to do and enjoy: Identify the overlap between your skills, interests, and market demand. Focus your job search on opportunities within this "sweet spot" to align passion with practicality.
> - **Realize that clarity is crucial for career success.** Use *The Focus List Exercise* to shape your job search and long-term career path. Avoid scattershot applications. Be deliberate and focused in your job search.

HOW I'LL APPLY THIS

CHAPTER 3:

Paint Your Store

(Build Your Personal Brand)

Once you know yourself and you've committed to staying focused, it's time to take action! I challenge you to embrace this unconventional path to success and watch as opportunities unfold before you.

In this chapter we start to build your personal brand—one that aligns with your skills and passions—by painting your store.

Follow these steps, but be sure to apply your own unique colors and style to your personal storefront.

Create an LLC . . . Yes, Start a Business! (Not Crucial, but Helpful)

In Chapter 1, I said to take your career portfolio and put it under an umbrella of sorts to make it legit. A limited liability company (LLC) is legit, huh?

If you're unclear about what to call it, name it something general to allow for your natural evolution. For example, my publisher started his LLC as Kory Kirby LLC. Over time he filed two DBAs ("doing business as" designations) for KORY KIRBY BOOKS® and Little Cabin Press, which are his full-time gigs now. He also has LinkedIn business pages for both these "companies" (more on this below).

Name it something that represents your work, your expertise, and your journey. Create a strong foundation that shows you're always moving forward, always growing, and always building your value. Own it, because that's your business.

And when I say *business*, I mean it.

It'll be helpful for you to establish your own LLC and proudly display it on your LinkedIn profile. Build a professional company page for it, adding legitimacy to your work history. Once you do this, you'll always have a job. You'll never have a dreaded employment gap, even if you're between roles. Your "consulting" business serves as a safety net, ready to be revisited when the time is right.

Create & Optimize Your LinkedIn Profile

I'll start by assuming you don't have a LinkedIn profile and take you all the way to advanced LinkedIn optimization strategies.

- **Create your account.** If you don't have a LinkedIn profile, it's time to create one. It's an essential step for building your professional online presence.
- **Claim your custom URL.** Ideally it's linkedin.com/in/your-name. If your name is taken, like mine was, adapt and do your best to make it simple: linkedin.com/in/wcraigfisher.
- **Use a professional photo.** Upload a clear, high-quality headshot. It should be well lit and showcase you.
- **Choose your banner.** Create a clear, high-quality, strategic banner image that reflects your brand and goals.
- **Select your headline.** Your headline is crucial, as it is

the first thing people see. Use keywords related to your industry or the job you're seeking, not just your job title. For example, instead of "Software Engineer," you could write "Software Engineer | Specializing in AI and Machine Learning." LinkedIn's search algorithm favors profiles with strong keywords.

- **Fill in your About information.** Write a concise summary that highlights your skills, experience, and what you bring to the table. Add a personal touch by sharing three things about you to make you more human. Let people get to know you a little bit, as you want them to connect with you on a personal level and get a sense of who you are beyond your professional experience. To boost visibility even more, strategically place a paragraph at the bottom with keywords, locations, your name, and your company's name. This technique, known as keyword stacking, allows you to dominate search results.[3] For example, when someone searches for terms like "employer brand strategy" or "LinkedIn training" AND "Dallas, Texas," my profile will appear at the top—my search engine optimization (SEO) and branding game on point.
- **Populate the Featured area.** Showcase key links, media, and projects. This is a great place to put a call to action (CTA).
- **Supply your experience.** For each job, write a brief description that highlights your achievements and the value you added. Use bullet points to make it easy to read. Again, use

---
3 LinkedIn not only approved of this "keyword stacking strategy" but embraced it as an internal best practice called "job tagging." They recognized its brilliance and asked us to teach it to all their salespeople. In fact, at the LinkedIn Talent Connect Conference, we even created the "Pimp My Profile" station. We dress up as car mechanics, offering fifteen-minute tune-ups for attendees' LinkedIn profiles. Executives lined up around the building to get their profiles optimized. LinkedIn now calls this "Rock Your Profile."

keywords in your "job titles," and view them as additional "headlines." These bolded sections on your LinkedIn profile are like the headlines on any web page—they catch the attention of search engines. The text itself is important, too, but those bold areas should contain keywords specific to your expertise and the kind of opportunities you want to pursue. Just like in your About section, strategically place a keyword paragraph at the bottom of each job experience.

- **Fill in your education.** Include your educational background, relevant courses, and any certifications you have earned. And, of course, use those keywords!
- **List your skills.** List skills that are most relevant to your industry and role. LinkedIn allows you to feature up to fifty skills.
- **Supply recommendations and endorsements.** Encourage colleagues and peers to endorse your skills and leave you recommendations to build credibility.
- **Apply SEO principles to your LinkedIn profile.** Craft a compelling story, infuse it with a touch of personalization, and strategically use keywords. By doing so, you'll enhance your personal branding and elevate your search ranking. When people are looking for professionals like you, they'll find you at the top of the results, standing out from the crowd.
- **Leverage your brilliant profile.** By implementing the strategies outlined above, your LinkedIn profile will radiate excellence. Your professional identity will be clear, and your value proposition will shine through. As people start to understand what you do and witness your valuable contributions, they'll be more inclined to connect with you.

Create a LinkedIn Business Page

Anyone can create a LinkedIn business page. It doesn't cost a thing! Why would you want to do this? A couple of reasons. If you're in transition, and you're telling people you're in transition, you are less likely to get a job than if you're currently employed. A lot of recruiters are starting to offer the following advice: "Stop saying you're in transition." Which is what I'm saying as well. Create your own thing.

My thing is TalentNet Media. It all started with my conferences in 2009. Then I incorporated my whole conference concept into a consulting business for employers in 2011. I created a LinkedIn business page so that I can have that on my profile, under my experience, and have it look like a legitimate place of work, because it has an icon, right? And you go to the page and it actually tells all about me and what my company does. There are lots of keywords on that page. What's cool about LinkedIn business pages is that they get outstanding SEO. And so if someone goes to search for "employer brand strategy Dallas, Texas," they're likely to find the TalentNet Media page from LinkedIn at the top of their Google search results.

So create a LinkedIn business profile for that LLC you created and named. Write about what you do. And, voilà, you'll never have a gap in your experience.

And if an employer has a problem with that, just say, "Hey, that's my side business. I do quilting on the side, macramé." Everyone has a gig. Everyone has a side project, and fewer and fewer employers have a real problem unless you're directly competing with them. And you don't have to ever close that page—it's your *store*, and you're going to want to keep it open.

Get Creative & Innovative—You Are the SME of You!

Your LinkedIn profile is not a legally binding document of any kind. In that vein, get creative and innovative with *you*—after all, you are the SME of you!

Add a New "Job" on LinkedIn

When I published my book *Hiring Humans* in September of 2023, I added a new "job" to my LinkedIn profile:

You know what happens when you add a new job on LinkedIn? LinkedIn tells everybody to congratulate you on your new job. Your entire network gets notified.

So suppose your new job is "In Transition" at "YourCompany.com," or whatever you're going to call your new business page. Or how about this?

- I'm your next greatest hire at [whatever your company's name is].
- Or SME at XYZ skill.

You can, for free, easily notify your entire network about this. And then they have a page (your storefront) to go to that's you being the SME of that thing you want to do and be.

It's also easy to point to. A lot of job applications are asking for other links about you. Or a portfolio. A LinkedIn business page is a great place for this.

Change Your Current Job Title

Another hot tip: Change your current job title. You can make it anything you want, right? If you're doing a temporary job, change your current job title to the following:

"I'm temporarily doing this until I go to work for Oracle." (If you want to go to work for Oracle, for example.)

Be sure to turn on "notify network" when you update your job title. As above, your entire network will get notified to congratulate you on your new job title.

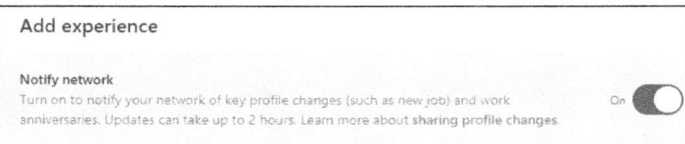

Beyond Your Digital Presence

Personal brand is commonly mistaken as the direct equivalent of your social media and digital presence. But it goes far beyond that. Personal brand is not just about self-promotion or being visible online; it's identifying who you are as a leader, how you treat people, and how you want to be known. In and out of the office.

Final Thoughts

By combining an optimized LinkedIn profile with a professional LLC and creative self-branding strategies, you can position yourself as a sought-after expert, maintain credibility during transitions, and stand out in a competitive job market.

> **KEY TAKEAWAYS**
> - **Start your LLC, optimize your LinkedIn profile, and create a LinkedIn business page.** This is foundational to everything else. Be sure to do this and do it first.
> - **Be creative with your LinkedIn presence.** Leverage LinkedIn's unique features and notifications.
> - **Treat your LinkedIn profile and business page as your storefront.** Position yourself as the SME and maintain an engaging and professional online presence.
> - **Go beyond your digital presence.** Your "in-person" reputation matters. Lead with integrity and treat others with respect.

HOW I'LL APPLY THIS

CHAPTER 4:

Take the Leap!

(Use *The L.A.K.E. Approach*)

Okay, so you see that the modern job hunt has evolved, and you know you're the CEO and it's full-time. You've answered foundational questions such as *Who are you? What do you do?* and *What's unique about you?* You've used *The Focus List Exercise* to help shape your long-term career path. You're building your personal brand by painting your store (LLC, LinkedIn profile, LinkedIn business page), and you're treating this all as your storefront (a vibrant display that tells the world who you are, what you offer, and why they should step inside).

I know you're reading this because you want a job. A new job. Perhaps your first job? Or you're looking to pivot and do something different. Well, it's time to take the leap and zero in on your job hunt.

Imagine Yourself Looking Across a Lake

Where you want to be is on the other side of the lake. You can't get there quickly. You don't have a boat, and you can't swim or jump across. It's too far. You can't walk, because it's too deep. You have to go around the lake to get there.

How would you get there?

Use *The L.A.K.E. Approach*

How would you get there? Well, you use L.A.K.E.: Look, Adjacent, Know, Engage.

Look
Where you want to go and the type of role or industry you aim to transition into.

Adjacent (Something Next to Something Else)
Think about adjacent situations with your recent employers or work situation.

Here are some questions to get you started:

- What's right next to you?
- What companies or roles are closely connected to your current or previous experiences?
- What companies would benefit from your knowledge, from the recent things you've been paid (or self-assigned) to do?
- Any competitors or vendors (to your former companies)?
- How about customers (of your former companies)?

These are organizations that would appreciate your knowledge—as *they're adjacent to what you've recently done.*

When you start finding these companies, you can use them to go around to other potentially more ideal companies.

What are five dream companies you'd love to work with?

1. _____
2. _____
3. _____
4. _____
5. _____

Know

Research the companies and opportunities identified in the adjacent step. Understand their needs, challenges, and the ways your skills align with their goals.

Write and document this research. Compare and contrast the five that you've chosen, even if they're radically different. Explain in your theory, or your thesis, that "I'm doing research on these companies because I would like to work for them."

State how they all approach the thing that I would like to do for work. Craft a captivating case study from your research that showcases your expertise and the ways you can make a difference for them. Publish your research on LinkedIn. Post it on your personal profile, and then repost to your company page (or vice versa).

By showcasing your expertise and genuine interest, it will resonate with your network and position you as a valuable contributor.

Engage

Instead of mindlessly applying to job postings and waiting for responses, take a more proactive approach:

- **Actively connect with key decision-makers and representatives.** Identify professionals on LinkedIn who hold positions relevant to where you're looking. Build relationships

with the people who might hire you to do some of the work that you'd like to do and that you're likely to get paid to do.
- **Paint your store—one post at a time.** Begin to post content. Think of every piece of content you create as a brushstroke in the masterpiece of your professional brand. (See the Tools & Tech section at the end of this book for my favorite content tools.)

Rest easy knowing your storefront is a vibrant display that tells the world who you are, what you offer, and why they should step inside.

Engage with other content, comment, and be an active participant in conversations. Cultivate a human connection and encourage your network to engage with your posts (callback to "Know"). This engagement will catch the algorithm's attention and boost the visibility of your content on the news feed.

As you create and post more content, tag all the people you've been connecting with at these companies to say the following:

"Hey, look what I did. I would love to do this for you."

Be the SME of you! This is something that no one else is doing. It would be rare, so be rare!

And when you post, be sure you're regularly posting video. Why?

Videos on LinkedIn Get Twenty Times More Shares Than Any Other Type of Content[4]

How many of you are regularly posting videos to your LinkedIn profile? Probably not enough.

---

[4] Laura Chaves, "20+ Exciting LinkedIn Video Statistics for Marketers (2024)," vidico.com, October 30, 2024, accessed February 28, 2025, https://vidico.com/news/linkedin-video-statistics/.

And that's a missed opportunity. Let's be clear: Videos on LinkedIn get twenty times more shares than any other type of content—twenty times! So if you're posting only text, sure, you'll get some engagement. Add a photo? You'll get more. But add a video? Now we're talking about real impact. That's why video is crucial.

How many of you have applied for a job that required a video? Some of you, right?

Employers love one-way video interviews because they can quickly assess candidates. But let's flip that. Why wait for a company to ask for a video? You can—and should—be posting your own. Every week, get on LinkedIn and document what you're up to. Post about the projects you're working on, talk about the research you're doing, or even share your job-search strategies. You can show off the way you track opportunities, the tools you're using, and so on. It's like creating a running portfolio of your expertise and thought process. The more people see you, the more they'll want to connect with you.

I recently checked out a tool, Cnect at Cnected.com (pronounced like "connect"), that lets you do just that—create a profile and record an intro video that cuts through the first round of interviews. I've seen hiring managers decide within seconds after watching these videos. They might look at a résumé and feel uncertain, but the moment they see a strong video, they're sold. Video gives them a taste of how you'll handle an interview or even a work meeting. It's the edge you need.

Sidenote: Check out Opus Pro (https://www.opus.pro/). This AI-driven platform is a game changer for enhancing your content's impact. Opus Pro allows you to create standout videos with dynamic visuals, captions, and effects. It even uses AI to help you optimize your content for social media algorithms, ensuring it performs well across platforms. Be sure to use Opus Pro's tools to auto-generate captions, which improve accessibility and engagement.

And don't worry about making your videos perfect. The goal is to publish. Sure, take the time to make it good—but don't overthink it. Once you get comfortable, batch your videos. Record a few at once on different topics, and then schedule them out. If you're not sure what to say in the post, here's a hack: Run the transcript through ChatGPT, get a blurb, and then clean it up. But don't rely too much on the tool—always add your personal touch.

One last tip: 80 percent of video content is watched with the sound off,[5] so captions are nonnegotiable. If you're uploading directly to LinkedIn, they'll even generate captions for you. Stick with vertical video too. It looks better on mobile, which is how most people are scrolling.

Videos are key for standing out on LinkedIn. Keep it simple, keep it regular, and let the world see you in action.

Your next opportunity could be one video away.

And, remember, it's not just about asking; it's about giving.

5:1 Give-to-Ask Content Ratio

Give, Give, Give, Give, Give: Ask.

The 5:1 give-to-ask ratio is an essential concept to keep in mind when you're looking to network your way to your next job. It's a fundamental principle based on the idea that in order to get something from someone, you have to give them something first. You can't keep asking for favors or making requests without giving something of value in return. It's like building a

---

[5] Laura Chaves, "20+ Exciting LinkedIn Video Statistics for Marketers (2024)," vidico.com, October 30, 2024, accessed February 28, 2025, https://vidico.com/news/linkedin-video-statistics/.

bank account of goodwill with your audience or network, and you need to make sure you have enough deposits before you start making withdrawals.

This principle is especially important when it comes to job seeking, as it's all about building relationships and trust with employers. You can't just post "looking for a job" and expect employers to recruit you. You need to make sure that you're building a relationship with your audience first and that you're providing value to them on a consistent basis.

That's where the 5:1 give-to-ask ratio comes in. The idea is to give value to your network five times before making an ask. This means that for every five pieces of content you post or actions you take to provide value to your audience, you can make one ask. This ratio ensures that you're not bombarding your audience with requests and that you're building trust and credibility with them.

Strive to provide value and contribute regularly. Aim for a ratio of five helpful contributions for every ask.

Catalyze Meaningful Projects

As you build connections and engagement, seize opportunities to collaborate on small projects or workshops. Your expertise and unique approach will capture attention, leading to more substantial projects and even full-time positions.

Remember, activity begets activity, and before you know it, you'll have a thriving practice, delivering exceptional work for the companies you've always wanted to work with.

This approach far surpasses the mundane act of submitting countless job applications. Recruiters might tell you to apply to three to five jobs a day, but this innovative concept propels you directly into conversations with your potential customers or employers, and it will set you apart in a refreshing and remarkable way.

Final Thoughts

As you zero in on your job search, *The L.A.K.E. Approach* is another tool in your tool kit. By focusing on adjacent opportunities, leveraging video, and consistently providing value, you can build trust, stand out, and navigate toward your ideal role effectively.

Just know that *The L.A.K.E. Approach* isn't a whole lot of help if your storefront doesn't look that good, *right?* That's why the first three chapters of this book are dedicated to this first. But by no means does this work in a vacuum. To build a vibrant display that's inviting, memorable, and reflective of your unique strengths, and which will ultimately attract the right opportunities and connections, all of this has to be working together. That's what painting your store is all about. So do it with care and creativity for lasting success.

> **KEY TAKEAWAYS**
> - **Visualize your career transition as a journey across a lake.** You cannot jump or swim directly to your destination—you must go around strategically using adjacent opportunities.
> - **Embrace L.A.K.E.** Look, Adjacent, Know, Engage.
> - **Look.** Envision where you want to go. Identify your ideal role, industry, or dream companies. Clearly visualize your end goal to maintain focus and direction.
> - **Adjacent.** Consider what adjacent opportunities provide a more accessible path to your ideal job. Leverage connections to roles or companies closely related to your experience.
> - **Know.** Conduct research on your target companies and document your findings. Compare and contrast. Create and publish case studies showcasing your insights.

Share and post on LinkedIn. Position yourself as a valuable contributor.
- **Engage.** Actively build relationships with key decision-makers at target companies. Post thoughtful content on LinkedIn, engage in discussions, and tag your connections to highlight your expertise.
- **Create video.** Use video content to stand out. Video on LinkedIn gets twenty times more shares than text or photos. Post regularly—document your projects, research, and job-search journey. Add captions, as 80 percent of videos are watched without sound. Use tools like Cnect (www.cnect.ai) or Opus Pro to create polished videos and save time.
- **Understand that consistency is key.** Keep it simple, batch-create content, and maintain a consistent posting schedule. Create a content calendar and repurpose content. Plan your posts in advance, mixing up your "Give" and "Ask" content. Use platforms like Trello, Asana, or Google Calendar to stay organized. A great video can also be turned into a blog post, LinkedIn article, or infographic. Don't reinvent the wheel—make your content work harder for you.
- **Honor the 5:1 give-to-ask content ratio.** Provide value to your network five times (via posts, helpful content, or engagement) before making one request. This ratio ensures you're not overwhelming your audience with requests and establishes trust and credibility.
- **Catalyze meaningful projects.** Collaborate on small projects to showcase your expertise and unique approach, building momentum toward larger opportunities and full-time roles. Activity begets activity.

CHAPTER 5:

The Content Blueprint—10 Lessons from a 700K-Follower Recruiter

(Featuring Guest Writer Joel Lalgee)

Content is the paintbrush you use to craft your professional brand and showcase your expertise. It's how you position yourself as an SME in your field. Whether you're writing posts, creating videos, or sharing insights, the tools you choose and the strategies you implement play a crucial role in your success.

I know that posting content online can be intimidating and challenging, especially in a professional context. So I asked Joel Lalgee to weigh in and provide some advice.

Joel Lalgee is an internationally known recruitment leader and coach who has helped thousands of recruiters build their brands online. In 2015, Joel started recruiting for a small start-up agency in Milwaukee. He quickly found his passion for recruitment. In 2019 he discovered content marketing, publishing his first posts on LinkedIn. Since then he has grown to over 257,000 followers on LinkedIn, 268,000 followers on TikTok, and 247,000 followers on Instagram. His content has been seen over two billion times. In 2023 he launched a media company that specializes in generating awareness for companies in the human resources / talent acquisition (HR/TA) space as well as consulting and training companies on how to grow on social media.

—

#1—It's a Small World

Regardless of what industry you're in, it's small. Your reputation has a way of traveling faster than you think. It's easy to forget that behind every single profile/account there's actually a person. If you are in an industry, you're probably going to meet them at some point. Your actions leave lasting impressions that can open doors or shut them. Also, what's online is not one thing and the real world another. They are the same. Your integrity and how you treat others are your most valuable currencies. So it's good to be asking yourself . . .

#2—What Do I Want to Be Known For?

I'm *The Realest Recruiter*. I want to be known for being real about recruiting and job searching. I want to put out authentic, no-BS content to help demystify recruiting and job searching.

But the reality is that it took me many years to get to this point. I only got here by . . .

#3—Being Bold and Taking Action

When I was in college, I wanted to make some money, so I got a finance degree.

I ended up going into a banking type of role, and it wasn't for me. I remember my dad walking into the bank and seeing me in a full suit and being like, "What . . . wait, this isn't you."

I then fell into recruitment through a personal connection.

(Which is key when you're looking for a job. Who do you know and where do they work?)

I discovered I actually enjoyed it.

Five or so years into recruiting I realized I wanted to be more of an entrepreneur—a self-employed solopreneur-type person. I no longer fit the constraints of most companies. I'm pretty opinionated. I want to make decisions for myself. I'm not afraid of risks. I realize that not everybody is like this, but I was okay with taking the risk and going out on my own.

This is how content creation came about. I started posting online and realized that I enjoy this. It's a creative outlet for me. Of course, when I first started putting myself out there, I kind of looked like an idiot. But slowly, over time, I got better. I noticed other people tried to start and they couldn't keep the longevity. I stayed consistent and my following grew. It opened up an infinite amount of doors for my business, speaking, and branding.

So I took action with school, and I just went in a direction. I figured out that wasn't the right direction. I took a pay cut to get into recruitment through a friend. I realized I'm okay at this and that I enjoy it. Then I went out on my own, to do the thing I really love, and started scaling up the content. Which got me to where I am today.

Action will teach you everything. When you take action, a lot of times you ~~fail~~ (learn). Our culture has a weird thing with failure. We look at failure as this really, really scary thing. And I think a lot of that's pride, but with failure, that's really the only way that you can learn.

So be bold, take action, do, and experiment. The worst that's going to happen is you're going to learn. If you don't take action, then you're in regret. You're always thinking, *I wish I would have done that* . . .

And while all this is unfolding before you, be sure to stay . . .

#4—Patient

I see massive pressure on people to figure out what they want to do for the rest of their lives—*right away*. But there are stages to it.

There's a guy I know who five years ago was an hourly worker at Domino's. He was thirty years old. He wasn't in a place in life that he wanted to be. So he took a developer course and worked really, really hard. He started posting on LinkedIn. He networked and applied to jobs. He got a job and worked his way up. Now he's an engineering manager at a tech company. He's got a huge social media following, which has opened up a lot of speaking and other opportunities. Now he's in a position where he wants to be. If you looked at him today, you might say, "I wish I had that." But it was a five-year journey.

Regardless of whether you're looking for your first job, or your next job, or a career change that will take you in a different direction, you have to be patient.

You can't expect to get your dream job right away. There's a path. The first step is getting a position. Maybe not your dream company, but any position where you can get experience and work your way in and up.

If you're patient, it's much easier to be . . .

#5—Authentic

One of the things that people always say to me about my content is that I'm so authentic. "You're genuine. You're a real person." This is because I share who I am. I share vulnerabilities. But I wasn't like, "Oh, I'm *The Realest Recruiter* now, so I'm going to be authentic." I started in banking (inauthentic) and worked my way to recruiting (more authentic), and now, today, to running my own business (very authentic).

It took me a while to find who I am and own my authenticity.

Regardless of where you are in your journey, keep in mind that who you are is really your . . .

#6—Brand

What do people say about you when you work with them, work for them, or help them? That's your brand.

Your online presence should be a magnification of that. But your actual brand is what people think and say about you when they get done with your interaction.

Are they going to say, "Oh, that guy wasn't helpful. You know he was really all about himself." Or are they going to say, "Wow, that was really valuable. That was helpful."

If there's a difference between who you know you are (who you want to be) and your current brand, that's where you can start to work toward.

But be careful not to make a persona that's not authentically you. It sets up expectations for the wrong thing.

If you said, "I love and I really care about people," but when people meet you and you don't give them the time of day and are actually super quiet and introverted, there's a misalignment.

It doesn't mean you have to have everything perfect and figured out. You can still have aspirations of who you want to be. But you can't lose that authenticity behind it.

And it's okay if you're afraid to put yourself out there, because online . . .

#7—Authenticity Doesn't Mean Full Transparency

They are two different things. You can be authentic with who you are and what you share. But you don't have to share everything.

For example, Gary Vaynerchuk is very authentic, but he doesn't actually disclose a lot about his personal life.

It's okay to have boundaries, and, in fact, you should have boundaries. But in the things that you're sharing, you're being authentic.

You're being real in your interactions; you're being real with people.

But you still have to . . .

#8—Be Professional

Know what "professional" means in your industry. What's accepted in marketing might not go over well in finance.

Find thought leaders who are creating good content in your space and branding themselves and use them as a guide. Learn what you can from them.

You can't just go in and unleash everything that's going on in your life. You still have to be professional.

For example, the job search right now is brutal. It's really challenging. But you don't want to voice all your complaints of everything that's happening online.

Let's say you have a terrible experience with an interview. One way you could deal with that is tag the company, tag the recruiter, and call them out.

A better way is to post something like, "Hey, job seekers—I know it's a challenge. Here's the story of how I went through it, and here's how I dealt with it."

One way is calling people out and being really negative and

hostile. The other is telling a story, learning, growing, and being encouraging to others.

Both are authentic. Both impact your brand. Choose wisely. And try to always be . . .

#9—Consistent

Obviously who you are will evolve and change, and that's okay. But there should be consistency to your core values that create your brand and your authentic self that shows up online and in person.

Consistency is key—and consistently getting better. You can't keep doing the same thing. I see this all the time with content. People create content for five years and no one's engaging with it. That's because it hasn't gotten any better.

I produced eight videos a day for a year. That's four thousand videos. They got better as I posted more. Most people aren't going to do this, but that's why most people don't have hundreds of thousands of followers.

For you, it might not be worth the time. Your time could be better spent learning a technical skill. And you might have to do some of that on the weekend. You've got to make . . .

#10—Sacrifices

Because other people won't. When I look at a lot of successful people I've talked to, I've realized that a lot of them have made sacrifices. You have to weigh that for yourself. Is the sacrifice worth the outcome?

For you, is the answer, "Yep, totally is. I know I need to sacrifice some time with my family, doing my hobbies . . ."?

Or you might not be willing to sacrifice as much.

Either one is okay!

What's not okay is wanting to do something—or be

something—and thinking that it's going to happen without putting any sacrifice or work into it.

It's a mindset that can be a really frustrating place to be in. And, trust me, I've been there.

As long as you can be clear with what your priorities and your goals are, you can create whatever that success looks like to you.

I often tell people that the hardest job ever is finding a job. So while you're at it, go easy on yourself. It's hard!

#11—Bonus Bullets for Your Job Search

- Don't be negative about prior jobs, prior bosses, or the process. Red flags.
- Don't tell people what you're earning. Tell them what you're targeting.
- Don't be unprepared. Anytime you're having a conversation with a recruiter or hiring manager, you've gotta know about the company and the role. The biggest complaint we get from hiring managers is people showing up not knowing anything about the company or the role. And I get it—you're applying to a lot of jobs. You lose track of the jobs. So . . .
- Track your job search. When I meet with people, one of the first questions I ask is, "How many jobs have you applied to?" The people who are struggling the most don't have any idea of how many jobs they've applied to. Treat your job hunt like a sales pipeline. Keep track of key milestones: the applications you've submitted, callbacks received, and how far you've progressed in the hiring process. This will reveal patterns, such as getting callbacks but not getting past the interview phase, or not receiving responses at all from your applications. Once you know the bottleneck,

you can take steps to fix it. You can rewrite your résumé or prepare better for interviews.
- Follow through with follow-up. And not just after an interview but whenever you reach out to someone. Don't just do it once. Show them that you really want to talk to them.
- Keep your messages short. "Hey, I applied for this job. Is it still open?" As opposed to "Hey, I applied to this job. My background fits it completely. Here's why, here's why, here's my résumé. Can I be considered for the job?" People have short attention spans, and they're getting contacted by a lot of people. Keep it short.

—Joel

Connect with me on:
- *LinkedIn: linkedin.com/in/joellalgee*
- *TikTok: @the_realest_recruiter*
- *Instagram: @the_realestrecruiter*
- *And check out my website: therealestrecruiter.com*

KEY TAKEAWAYS

- **Reputation and integrity matter.** Your reputation in any industry travels fast. Treat others with respect and integrity, both online and offline, because both avenues are intertwined and leave lasting impressions that can open or close future opportunities.
- **Bold action drives growth.** Taking risks, experimenting, and learning from failure are essential for personal and professional growth. Action leads to clarity, while inaction leads to regret—embrace boldness and persistence to move forward.

- **Embrace patience and progression.** Career success often takes time and unfolds in stages. Start by gaining experience, even if it's not your dream role, and work your way up while staying patient and focused on long-term goals.
- **Authenticity is key.** Be true to yourself while remaining professional. Share your story and values honestly, but maintain boundaries and avoid oversharing. Authenticity builds trust and strengthens your personal brand.
- **Be consistent and sacrifice.** Success requires consistent effort and a willingness to make sacrifices. Whether it's time spent improving a skill or creating content, continuous improvement and alignment with your goals are critical to achieving your version of success.

HOW I'LL APPLY THIS

CHAPTER 6:

Document Every Great Outcome

(Have Evidence)

In the midst of all this work, your professional endeavors will pile up. Be it as an employee or an entrepreneur, it's crucial to capture the brilliance that unfolds. When a good idea strikes or someone praises your work, embrace the power of documentation. Follow these steps, my friend, and watch your achievements stack up.

Create a Google Document

Open up a Google document (or maybe a custom GPT), your digital canvas to preserve the greatness that unfolds. Keep a running list of all the remarkable things you've accomplished, accompanied by their outcomes. As these instances occur, take a screenshot of the positive outcome and paste it into your document. Take a moment to add a few notes and capture the essence of that achievement.

Cherish Feedback and Recognition

Whenever someone acknowledges your exceptional work, whether it's a colleague, a manager, or a client, capture it. Screenshot their kind words or add their name to the document so you can follow up with them later for a quote. These snippets of appreciation serve as invaluable testimonials to showcase your capabilities.

Leverage Your Documentation

As time passes and the company you work for approaches your quarterly review, you can employ this comprehensive document to confidently answer the question, "What have you done for me lately?" Showcase your list of accomplishments and highlight the positive outcomes you've generated. You'll have a treasure trove of case studies to reference, substantiating your value and contributions.

Benefit Your Consulting Business

If you're running your own consulting venture or pursuing other endeavors, having a document filled with your achievements is a game changer. When prospective clients inquire about references or examples of your work, you won't need to scramble or create new material. You can confidently say, "Yes, indeed. I have it all right here." Your extensive record of accomplishments will impress and reassure potential clients.

Most people overlook the importance of this simple practice. By embracing the power of documentation, you'll be well prepared to showcase your excellence, whether within a company or as an independent professional. Don't let your victories fade into the background. Embrace this habit, and you'll be grateful when the time comes to shine a light on your achievements.

KEY TAKEAWAYS

- **Create a running record of achievements.** Maintain a Google document to capture your accomplishments, accompanied by outcomes and screenshots of positive feedback or recognition.
- **Leverage documentation for reviews and opportunities.** Use your documented achievements as evidence of your value during performance reviews, job interviews, or client pitches, ensuring you're always prepared to showcase your contributions.
- **Transform feedback into testimonials.** Collect and save feedback from colleagues, managers, or clients to build a repository of testimonials that validate your skills and strengthen your professional brand.
- **Visit Mahalohub.com.** This tool allows you to request video testimonials from your customers or audience.

CHAPTER 7:

The Power of Networking, Referrals, and Stories

(Featuring Guest Writer Jim D'Amico)

Let me be real with you: The job search is tough. I know. I've been there, and I've seen it from every angle—candidate, recruiter, consultant. And if you're reading this, chances are you've spent some time navigating that maze of applications, automated systems, and what feels like radio silence from employers.

Don't rely solely on the résumé-submission process to get noticed. Instead, build your network, leverage referrals, and consistently show the world why you're the best person for the job.

Think of networking as your backstage pass. Sure, you could wait in the general admission line with thousands of other hopefuls—or you could use your connections to get in through the side door.

Here's the reality: Many jobs aren't even posted online.

But don't take it from me; take it from Jim D'Amico, whom I've called in to share his story and thoughts on networking, sharing referrals, and telling stories.

Jim is a globally recognized talent-acquisition leader

specializing in building best-in-class talent-acquisition functions for global organizations. He was named 2020, 2021, and 2022 Talent Innovator. He's also an author, speaker, and mentor with an intense passion for all things talent acquisition.

—

I started in the military, went to a military college, was in the military for eight years. I was a crewman in tanks in the army. Then, when I got out, there weren't a whole heck of a lot of civilian jobs.

I was a tanker with not a lot of *real-world* skills, and a degree in secondary education. I wanted to be a stand-up comedian. So I studied improvisational comedy. I toured doing stand-up. It was going to be my thing. It didn't work out for me. I had no idea what I was going to do.

But then I started looking at what I did have: tremendous discipline, a lack of fear, and the ability to tell very engaging stories.

Who needs that?

Sales.

In sales you've got to be disciplined, because it's all about numbers. You have to be fearless, because your life is rejection. And you have to always be able to have a good conversation with all types of people.

So I got into sales.

The company I was working for was bought by a competitor, and a friend of mine said, "Hey, I work for a recruiting company. Come work with me. You'll love it because you're selling two ends. The person on the company and the company on the person. It's a lot more fun."

So I went into this old-school boiler-room recruiting—smile-and-dial kind of recruiting. I loved it. I was good at it.

What I didn't like was the adversarial nature of it. It's me against the company. If they don't hire my candidate, I don't get paid. If I don't get paid, I don't eat. It's me against the candidate. If the candidate doesn't accept my offer, I don't get paid. I don't eat.

And so a mentor of mine at the time said, "Well, come work for me and let's build a better model."

We built an early version of recruitment process outsourcing (RPO).

After building that, I went in house to build a best-in-class TA function, and I developed the Differentiated Recruiting Model.[6]

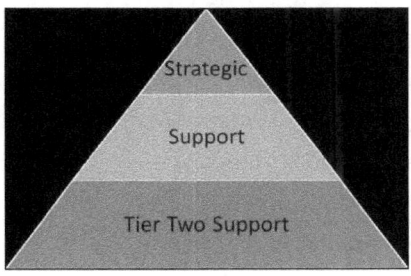

1. **Strategic roles** have direct and significant revenue generations or develop the strategy or technology to enable revenue generation.
2. **Support roles** directly enable strategic roles.
3. **Tier 2 support roles** provide necessary service to the company but do not necessarily enable revenue generation.

As an example, in many organizations, commercial sales is most likely a strategic role, talent acquisition is a support role, and custodial services is a Tier 2 support role.

---

6 Jim D'Amico, "Differentiated Recruiting Model," LinkedIn, November 27, 2017, accessed February 24, 2025, https://www.linkedin.com/pulse/differentiated-recruiting-model-jim-d-amico/.

That model has been highly effective, and I've spent many years teaching and implementing it.

And so when Craig asked me to contribute to this book, I was happy to throw my hat in the ring and give back to this community that's given me so much.

I'd like to start by addressing the common approach most job seekers take.

They mass apply to jobs and get dropped into the ATS. Which is sort of like throwing yourself into a black hole. It's tricky to stand out in the ATS alone, as most ATSs read keywords and skills that don't tell a story about you. And all too often they are gamed by keywords and skills. (In Chapter 8 we deep dive into the ATS.)

Recruiters are overworked and busy. So they're not taking the time to look at the applications or the résumés. Anything you've done to your résumé to stand out—they're not seeing. Which is why relying on a robot for your career is not the best.

Here's a better way.

Let's say you're in sales, but you want to get into marketing.

Don't spam strangers on LinkedIn: "Hey, can you refer me to this job?"

Network. Build real relationships. Focus on adding value, being curious, and showing genuine interest in the people in your industry. Try to understand the culture, ask thoughtful questions, and contribute to the conversation in meaningful ways. Share articles or insights that align with their interests. Become someone who is visible and helpful, not just another person asking for something.

Don't make it about you, make it about them.

For example, let's say you know Steve, the VP of marketing at company X that you'd like to work for. Or you don't know Steve! Never talked to him. Doesn't matter. Reach out and say something like, "Hey, I'm really interested in how people have built their sales career. I admire you and company X. I'd love to hear how you built your sales career. Could we grab fifteen minutes for a chat? It would be so fascinating to me."

Only jerks will say no—and you don't want to work for a jerk.

The reason this works so well is because people love to tell you about themselves. Then, because most humans learn good courtesy, they will also ask you about you. Once they open the door, you can start talking about your interests and goals. You can ask, "Hey, if I wanted to be in marketing in your organization, what would I need to do? What skills do you think that I would need? Who would I need to talk to?"

Even if you don't have the skills yet, you now have a list. You could go develop them.

So you do. And you keep talking to more people. You've officially opened yourself up to unexpected moments and opportunities.

Then one day you're talking to Joel. He's the marketing manager for company X, in the Southwest Region of the US (where you're based). You and Joel hit it off. You have a great call!

Joel says, "Hey, you should apply to this job that's open. I think you'd be a good fit. I'll tell the hiring manager, Wendy, about our call, and why I think you're a qualified candidate."

This bada boom, the human-to-human networking thing, just bypassed the ATS altogether. Instead of being lost in a black hole, you're now a *human*.

Someone who already works at the company has vouched for you. You've already bypassed the first hurdle—*trust*.

The hiring manager searches for you—the real human that her coworker recommended to her—finds your information, reaches out, and invites you for an interview.

This is 100 percent the way you should be navigating your job search.

As humans, we're relationship driven. This actually eases the process for everybody.

Think about it. We've changed the way we shop. Hiring is very similar to shopping. When you shop, you take recommendations as the most legit, credible, and, of course, *real*. If your friend and your cousin had a wonderful experience at Richardson Toyota, and they both recommend that you go there, and you're looking for a Toyota, aren't you going to go there?

Just like in hiring: "Hey, I know you're trying to hire a financial analyst. I know this guy Jim. He's perfect."

Done! Think about how much easier that is for both parties. It changes everything. When the recommendation comes from a trusted peer, *it's gold.*

Now, throughout your career, job search, and networking efforts, *lean into storytelling.*

Your Quiver of Stories

Have a quiver of stories at the ready at all times. Be ready at any moment to pull out and shoot a bull's-eye based on whatever question is asked of you.

And not just any stories, experiential stories that weave together the three elements of your career: who you've worked for, the results you've delivered, and your skills.

Most people talk about these three elements as independent things. What you need to be able to do is bring them together into experiences and craft stories around those experiences.

I teach a master class in storytelling, and the thing that I preach is the three-act method:

1. **Act One:** Context.
2. **Act Two:** Obstacle.
3. **Act Three:** Resolution.

In general, you're only going to have between thirty and ninety seconds to tell the story. I recommend first person for this type of thing.

Act one is setting the scene, and it's clearly setting the scene. So I might say, "Hey, Jim, I want to tell you about a time when I had to go out of my way to fix a broken process. At our company, we had a really bad process around how we manufactured widgets."

I've set the stage. Next, I'm going to tell Jim, "The challenge we had was we were under budget and had time constraints to fix this, and nobody else could figure it out."

The obstacle I had to overcome is clear.

Then I might say, "Look, I think we're overthinking the process. We're thinking end to end, but if we just change this one step, it's actually going to reduce our costs, reduce our errors, produce a better result, and we can do it in three days versus three months. So then that's how I solved it. That's the solution."

To do this, you're going to need to research the company and hiring manager (or whoever) to understand what's important to them. You can then tailor your stories to align with their values.

However . . . **never lie!**

Your quiver should be full of first-tier stories—how you've made money, saved money, or improved a process.

As well as second-tier stories—the why, the altruistic angle on why you do what you do, and what it is you do.

I'll give you an example.

So, again, you're in sales. I'm looking at hiring you for a marketing role.

I'm going to see that you're doing all the sales stuff. You are making calls, reaching out to prospects, doing presentations and proposals, all that jazz.

But that's not marketing. Marketing is different from sales.

You need to show me that you know how to do marketing.

So take your experience and craft a story around it. For example:

"I'm making the switch to marketing, as I think I'd be very good at it. Last year, I was interested in switching our programmatic vendor, since programmatic advertising wasn't working for us . . . I had to get buy-in from my peers and our users. I built a case study by reaching out to peers at similar companies, that clearly defined which vendors best serviced companies our size, and their track record of success. I showed how programmatic wasn't the problem; it was our mismatch with a vendor that focused on enterprise accounts and not small niche companies. I 'marketed' a new idea internally!"

This story was based on an experience that showed me that you can do what I, as the hiring manager, am looking for you to do in this role.

Now, you can say that "I can market," but until you show me . . . I'm skeptical.

Fill your quiver with stories. Pull them out during networking calls and use them in your interview process.

Show the world that you are the SME of your own story.

This is how you get "recruited" instead of always chasing down jobs.

Which is exactly what I've done in my career. It's been hard work, but it's worked quite well.

I didn't even interview for my last two jobs. There was a need, but not at my level. They created the roles for me because they wanted me. I "applied" once they created the job. But this was only to get my information in their system. You know, provisioning—background check, payroll, business card, office name—all that stuff.

As Craig would say, this is because I *painted my store*. I didn't even think about my résumé for these roles. Back in the day, of course I did—but now, with my brightly colored storefront, I didn't put much thought into it at all.

No one cared what was on there. They already know and trust me.

But it took years of me honing my craft. Sales. Stories. Recruiting. I developed the Differentiated Recruiting Model. It's been proved credible over and over again. I've written and spoken about it tons of times. I've created content and an online persona. My teams have had success.

All this takes time. So settle in and enjoy the ride.

The first thing I do when I get out of bed is say, "I'm going to make today a good day to die." That's my goal every day. If I get hit by a bus, or if I drop dead, then I die proud.

Perspective is a good friend. Keep it close. And do what you can to approach every day as if it's your last.

I'm rooting for you.

—*Jim*
Connect with me on:
- *LinkedIn: linkedin.com/in/jimdamico*

KEY TAKEAWAYS

- **Embrace networking over applications.** Relying solely on submitting hundreds of applications doesn't work well. Don't waste your time talking to the machine. Talk to people. Focus on building genuine relationships with people in your target companies. Networking acts as your "backstage pass," giving you access to hidden opportunities and bypassing the competitive bottleneck.
- **Understand that referrals are game changers.** Referred candidates often receive priority because they bring built-in trust and credibility. Build connections by engaging thoughtfully with employees of your target companies on LinkedIn or at industry events, then position yourself as a strong fit before requesting a referral.
- **Use storytelling for professional branding.** Mastering storytelling and using a three-act structure (context, obstacle, resolution) help job seekers communicate their unique value. Experiential stories should highlight key accomplishments, impact, and transferable skills tailored to prospective roles.
- **Know that personal branding + networking = success.** Combine strategic networking with a strong personal brand as an SME. By consistently engaging and showcasing your expertise, you increase your visibility and credibility, making it more likely for hiring managers to think of you for future opportunities or reach out directly.

Chapter 7: The Power of Networking, Referrals, and Stories

HOW I'LL APPLY THIS

CHAPTER 8:

Applying to Jobs

(The ATS Is Not Your Enemy)

If you've been asked to submit a résumé, and you're not Jim, you have to put some time, thought, and intention into it. This and the next chapter are for you.

All right, so you've been tasked with submitting a résumé for a job application. This means that your résumé is about to enter the ATS, which gets a lot of buzz and is often misunderstood by job seekers. So before we dive into résumé writing (Chapter 9), I wanted to cover a few important things.

Empathy Goes Both Ways

There's a growing realization among companies that candidates are not just numbers—they're potential team members. So I like to say, "If you've applied for a job, you've done some work for that company." And you should expect to be treated with the respect that comes with that.

But here's the thing: Empathy goes both ways. As a job seeker, you need to understand that hiring managers and recruiters are navigating their own challenges too. They're working with limited resources, often juggling multiple open positions and dealing with systems that aren't perfect. That's why it's so important to approach the application process with empathy and patience.

Understanding the ATS

First things first: What is the ATS? The ATS is software used by employers to manage applications and streamline the hiring process. It helps recruiters sift through hundreds, sometimes thousands, of résumés and identify the best candidates quickly.

I know what you're thinking: "But, Craig, doesn't that mean the ATS is just a faceless robot throwing my résumé into a black hole?" Not exactly. The ATS is just a tool—an imperfect one, sure—but a tool that does a job. Its role is to scan your résumé for keywords and qualifications that match the job description. Yes, it's automated, and, yes, that can feel impersonal.

Dealing with the dreaded ATS is one of the biggest frustrations job seekers face today. I've heard the complaints, and I've lived through them myself. But here's a truth that might surprise you.

The ATS is not your enemy.

When you shift your perspective and realize that the ATS is not out to sabotage your job search—and neither are the recruiters or hiring managers—it changes the game. You stop seeing the process as a battle to be won and start thinking of it as a conversation to be had.

Now, before you roll your eyes and skip ahead, hear me out. I'm not saying ATSs are perfect. In fact, some are downright frustrating. But they are getting better. And, more important, the ATS is just one piece of the puzzle. Don't let it define your entire experience.

If you combine strategic networking with a strong personal brand, you'll find that doors start opening in ways you never expected. The goal is to make yourself irresistible—to both the system and the people behind it. Remember, the best candidates aren't just found; they're the ones who make themselves impossible to miss. If you approach the application process with the right mindset and strategy, it can actually work for you, not against you.

It's Not Just the ATS

Let's not give the ATS more credit—or blame—than it deserves. It's just one piece of the candidate journey. The truth is that your experience as a job seeker goes far beyond an automated system.

From the moment you hit "Apply," your experience with an employer begins. And as someone who's helped employers audit and refine their candidate experience for years, I can tell you that *how* you experience that journey matters just as much as *whether* you get the job. Employers are starting to understand this too. They know that if their hiring process is slow, clunky, or dehumanizing, they risk turning off great talent before they even get a chance to interview them.

This is why you're seeing more companies investing in tools that improve communication, speed up the process, and—yes—help the ATS do a better job of identifying top talent. The ATS isn't going anywhere, but employers are realizing they need to put the *human* back in human resources.

The human element is what makes all the difference, so be sure to bring that into writing your résumé!

KEY TAKEAWAYS

- **Empathy goes both ways.** Job seekers should be patient with recruiters' challenges, while employers must treat applicants with respect and care throughout the process.
- **The ATS is a tool, not the enemy.** If you approach the application process with the right mindset and strategy, the ATS can actually work for you, not against you.
- **The candidate experience matters.** To attract top talent, employers are recognizing the need to make the hiring process faster, more human, and more engaging.

HOW I'LL APPLY THIS

CHAPTER 9:

Résumés That Recruiters Love— Inside Secrets for Landing Your Dream Role

(Featuring Guest Writer Trish Wyderka)

To help you write a résumé that recruiters love, land your dream role, and work with the ATS, I've called in Trish Wyderka for her expertise.

Trish is a talent sourcer (a professional who finds potential candidates for a job), who has worked in recruiting for fourteen years. Each and every day her brain is hyper focused on where she can find people with X skills for Y role. She's also a résumé writer who has looked at hundreds of thousands of résumés in her role as the database administrator for the ATS at her company. So she knows what she's looking for.

—

Before my career in recruiting, I was in the air force. The funny thing is that when I was leaving the air force and searching for a job, a recruiter said my résumé looked terrible. And you know what? I had no idea what that meant! I struggled to get jobs and I hated recruiters. So when I accidentally found myself in recruiting, I was determined to do better.

I took time to help people, even when they weren't qualified (providing advice on what they could fix on their résumé to get seen). Unlike that recruiter who just said mine was terrible, I wanted to contextualize things and help people. I even wrote an article titled "Recruiters, We Can Do Better." All it takes is a few minutes to give someone advice about their résumé. I've done my best to stick with this. And so here I am, a résumé writer for all these years and working in recruiting. It's just phenomenal. So when Craig asked me to provide some advice on résumés, I was excited about the chance to keep giving back and trying to do better.

Before we get to the good stuff, I have a few important notes for you:

- This advice from a recruiting point of view will help you understand what we recruiters are thinking and looking for.
- There are many different opinions out there. These tips have been tried and tested with my clients.
- Résumés vary by industry, role, and the job seekers' career experience, skills, and goals. You will want to ensure that your résumé is geared toward the position you are applying for.
- I specialize in senior-level federal and civilian résumés because I'm prior air force. I've done more than three hundred federal résumés alone in the last three years. I'm passionate about helping federal and military people just getting out, because civilian recruiters and hiring managers do not understand our background.
- And last, everything listed here is for US-based professionals.

With that context in place, I'm going to paint with broad strokes, focusing on key themes to help you craft a résumé that recruiters will love. Here we go!

Be Cautious with "Résumé Professionals"

If you've sent out numerous résumés, hired a résumé writer, reworked your entire résumé, and ensured it's ATS compliant but still aren't getting interviews, you may have received incorrect advice.

You see, I've reviewed countless résumés that were supposedly written by "résumé professionals." The problem becomes apparent quickly: These writers often lack actual recruiting experience or industry insight. Instead of creating truly compelling content, they typically just rearrange existing information and make minor wording changes before collecting their fee. But consistently missing are the crucial elements that make a résumé stand out: quantifiable achievements and value-driven bullet points that demonstrate real impact and differentiation. I can see this in two seconds right at the beginning. "Wow, you're a VP, and it says you work well and can get along with your team. Well, of course you should! You're a VP." I want to see some numbers, percentages and dollar signs. But I often don't see it, and I don't know why these "résumé professionals" aren't helping with this.

Be Cautious with "AI Generators"

The other thing I see is too many people relying on AI generators like ChatGPT, which is terrible for entire résumés. AI doesn't know you, and it's guessing on the value you provided. It never knows your specific impact on an organization. Sure, tweak a line here or there, but not the whole thing. I NEVER see AI add quantifiable value-driven information, not to mention the grammar is just sloppy robotics.

People seem to think it's a good idea to take job descriptions from their current job, or past jobs, put it through ChatGPT, and have it spit out their résumé. A job description tells what the job was about, not what you did. I want to know the quantifiable metrics and results that will inform your performance in this new job. Use the job description to inform your résumé, but don't use the description and AI for the whole thing.

You still have to put your heart and soul into your résumé and let them know, "Hey, this is what I can do."

Follow Instructions

It sounds obvious, but you'd be amazed at how many applications get tossed simply because the candidate didn't follow directions. If the job posting asks for a cover letter or specific attachments, make sure you include them.

Tailor Every Application

I know it's tempting to send the same résumé to multiple jobs, but the more tailored your résumé is to a specific role, the better your chances of making it through the ATS. Think of each résumé as a customized tool for each job.

Job Descriptions

I touched on this above, but outside of AI, this same logic still applies: Job descriptions tell what the job is about, not what you did. I don't want to know more about your past job; I want to know the quantifiable metrics and results that directly relate to this job.

If you're going to apply for a job, you should be able to do 80 percent or more of what's on the job description, and you should ensure those things are addressed in your résumé.

And pay attention to those little details. For example, if they want someone who knows QuickBooks, and you know QuickBooks, but you don't have it on your résumé, you're not going to get picked up in the ATS.

Use those important keywords. But don't overdo it. Keyword stuffing is a red flag for both the system and human recruiters.

Formatting

When résumés come in, they go through the ATS. Think of the ATS as a filing system. It's not something that is just screening people out; it's more like a holding system for résumés. It's like those old accordion file systems that you stored bills and receipts in. When the résumé comes in through the system, it looks like a simple text file, and it uploads. If you have your information formatted right, *it falls in*. If it's wrong, *it doesn't fall in*.

Considering I'm the ATS database administrator, you'd be surprised at how many résumés I have to fix so that we can read them. Putting your résumé in a weird template or overdesigning it results in a wonky document that won't make it through the ATS. You want a simple font and layout, and only a few headers so that the ATS can scan your résumé and extract the information on you (name, phone number, email, LinkedIn, etc.).

Follow these general guidelines to ensure your résumé *falls in*:

- File type: Use Microsoft Word or Google Docs. If you don't have Word, use Google Docs and download it as a PDF or a Word document. Be sure you check which file formats are accepted. Not all companies and ATSs like PDFs. You might need to upload a .doc or .docx file.

- Font: Calibri.
- Text: 10 point.
- Columns: one.
- Justification: full. Look for large white gaps between the words and note the page breaks. Depending on how the text appears, adjust the margins to 0.6" or even 0.7". Ensure the text is properly aligned.
- Headers: all caps, 11 point, bold.
- Subheads: sentence case, 10 point, bold.
- Job titles: italics.
- Bullets: plain black circles.
  - Sub-bullets: open circles.
    - And so on.
- No photos, tables, charts, or visuals of any kind.
- No running heads or footers.

It's okay to have another version that's a bit more designed and maybe colored. Different font. Jazzed up a bit for a direct email to someone. Or printed out on thicker paper for an in-person occasion. Just be careful about its journey and where it's going, because everybody is using the ATS, and you'd hate to be thrown out simply for formatting. If your industry is creative and graphic design oriented, then of course follow your industry's standards.

Writing & Structure

The beginning of your résumé is the most important. It's where the bulk of these issues arise. Follow this structure, from top to bottom:

1. Position You're Applying For

Put the job title of the position you are applying for at the top.

Center it. Make it your main header. If your name is in the header, it won't flow in the ATS. So how am I supposed to see you?

2. Personal Information

Below goes your name, city and state, phone number, and email. This goes without saying, but you're only human. Get this information right. Don't put your address on your résumé. I'm not coming to your house for tea. Do feel free to put your LinkedIn or GitHub or whatever links are important. Just know you need to have it hyperlinked with "www."

3. Intro or Career Summary

Supply a quick snapshot of you and summary of the résumé. Open with your current title and years of experience in your industry. Then give four or five core competency examples with two to three impactful bullets. Both (or at least one) need to have a $ sign or % in it.

Something like this:

Senior Director with 12 years of experience in the automotive industry . . . (or track record of success includes . . .).

- Securing **$10M** in new business contracts, and optimizing cost efficiencies across global supply chains.
- Spearheading operational improvements that increased production efficiency by **35%** and reduced defects by **20%**, enhancing overall quality and compliance.

Think about what sets you apart from the other five hundred people. You want quantifiable examples of how you've helped a company make money, save money, or save time.

I often hear, "I don't make money for the company." But time is money. Let's say you took over a role as a secretary and your company didn't have to replace Susie, who just left. You've been doing it for one year. Assuming you were paid the same, what is the approximate amount of money that you saved the company from having to hire another admin?

I also hear from a lot of people that they don't have any stats or metrics. If you don't track your success metrics, now is the time to start! Think of going to ask your boss for a raise. Why should your boss give you a raise? Well, because you contributed XYZ amount of dollars a year, of course. I have metrics going back to 2013. The typical person doesn't. That sets me apart from the other five hundred people.

A recruiter should be able to read the intro in ten to thirty seconds. If they don't see any quantifiable value, they're not going to read the rest of your résumé.

4. Professional Experience

Add all relevant jobs from the past ten years. Title, name of company, work location, and dates (month and year). If you've had three or four jobs while at the same company, that's called career progression. Put the date when you started with the company. Then break out separate titles to delineate your progression. Include dates.

A few other things to keep in mind:

- Ask yourself, What kind of problems did I solve for the company? For example, "Identified a $3 million problem, and because I did that, I was able to save [impactful quantifiable metric]."
- What is impactful in my industry? For example, "Grew sales account from zero to $100,000 in nine months."

- If you did volunteer work or were a stay-at-home mom (or dad) but now you're doing this, that counts. So have that going back.
- Limit text to one sentence per bullet.
- The words *I*, *me*, and *my* should never appear in your résumé.

5. Other Professional Experience

Include all relevant jobs from the previous ten to fifteen years. List title, name of company, work location, and dates (month and year). You don't need to provide more information than this.

6. Education & Training

Include degree type, field of study, school, and graduation date. Be sure to include training, certifications, and courses.

7. Tools & Skills

Include important software and programs. List them out and include all the versions. Think keywords.

If you put down *"CRM Software,"* I'm like, What? If you put down *"Salesforce CRM,"* I'm like, Which module of Salesforce?

8. No References

I'm not a fan of references on a résumé. If I want references, I'll ask you for them.

Grammar

I have an editor review every résumé I work on for a final polish. I have found that this increases the chances of success. I had a boss once who said, "When I look at résumés, if I see spelling errors or tons of grammar issues, I'm not sending it on."

In your Word and Google Doc files, look for those red and blue underlines. Read through it and ask, "Does it make sense?" Think about logical flow. I don't want to see that you lead a team at the bottom of all the bullets. I want you to say, "Senior director leading a team of twenty, reporting to so-and-so."

Ask a colleague, trusted partner, friend, or family member to read it. Ask if they understand the big picture, the intro, and how that summarizes the rest.

One more important note: Let's say I'm looking for someone who works for IBM. It's helpful for my searching if you include both. If you're going to use acronyms, spell out the first one and then put the abbreviation in parentheses so you'll get pulled up.

Length

If you're a recent college graduate, a page or a page and a half is good. In general, aim for two pages. However, there are exceptions. For example, if you're in IT, technical, engineering, or federal industries, then you can go four to six pages. I always say that if you don't have it on your résumé, you never did it.

Three Important "Don'ts"

1. **Don't put your résumé on LinkedIn.** Do what Craig says to do with your LinkedIn.
2. **Don't use a ridiculous personal email.** I'm sorry, but shehoolahoops69@gmail.com isn't professional.
3. **Don't give up!** I once coached someone who was not qualified for the job they applied for, but because the résumé was written around their transferable skills and background, the company created a job for them. They were supposed to be an admin assistant. Instead, they created a new role

entirely, and they started at $16.80 an hour. Over the next decade they worked their way all the way to a six-figure salary in that company.

—Trish
Connect with me on:
- *LinkedIn: linkedin.com/in/trishwyderka*
- *And check out "Résumés by Trish" on Facebook: facebook.com/ResumesbyTrish*

> **KEY TAKEAWAYS**
> - **Be wary of résumé professionals and AI generators.** Many lack industry-specific recruiting experience and fail to include quantifiable, results-driven details. AI tools are useful for tweaks but should not write entire résumés, as they often miss impactful metrics.
> - **Follow instructions and tailor applications.** Customize your résumé for each job, align it with the job description, and ensure it meets application requirements like cover letters or specific file formats.
> - **Prioritize formatting for ATSs.** Use simple fonts, headers, and layouts compatible with ATSs. Avoid tables, graphics, or templates that might disrupt parsing.
> - **Structure résumés effectively.** (1) Position you're applying for, (2) personal information, (3) intro or career summary (must have $ sign or percentage in it), (4) professional experience (quantifiable), (5) other professional experience, (6) education and training, (7) tools and skills, (8) no references.
> - **Focus on results and metrics.** Showcase how you

saved time, increased revenue, or solved problems. Use industry-relevant keywords to highlight your impact and avoid vague, generic statements.
- **Proofread and polish.** Eliminate grammar and spelling errors, maintain logical flow, and have trusted individuals review your résumé for clarity and professionalism.
- **Adapt length and content.** Résumés should reflect your experience—typically two pages for most roles and longer for technical or federal positions.
- **Don't . . .** put your résumé on LinkedIn, use an unprofessional email, or GIVE UP!

HOW I'LL APPLY THIS

CHAPTER 10:

Impress, Don't Stress—A Human Approach to Job Interviews

(Featuring Guest Writer Erika Oliver)

Alright, so you've got a good-looking store and brand; you've established yourself as an SME of that thing you want to do and be; you've networked your way in, were invited to apply, and wrote a résumé that recruiters love; and you just got asked for an interview. Whew, yeah, that's a full-time thing there, right? Pause and pat yourself on the back. I'm proud of you.

I'm sure you've noticed the theme here. Be human, be yourself. Impress, don't stress! I've tapped Erika Oliver, a certified executive and career coach, to step in and guide you through the final mile of your job hunt.

Erika Oliver is a seasoned product leader and talent-acquisition strategist who brings a unique perspective to the intersection of talent, technology, and human potential. As an executive and career coach, she has dedicated her career to bridging the gap between employers and job seekers. Her deep commitment extends beyond traditional job placement—she focuses on guiding professionals toward roles that align with their core values and life aspirations, ensuring both individuals and organizations thrive.

—

I've interviewed countless people who seemed like strangers to their own true selves.

To be successful in an interview (and in your career), you have to be true to who you are, not to who people think you are, and not to who you wish to be.

If you can't answer the following question:

Who am I?

Then you need to. And don't worry if this question makes you uncomfortable and feels like a struggle. That only means you're human. Everyone struggles with this question at some point in their lives. Literally everyone.

That is why I always like to start here with my career coaching. Because if you aren't clear on who you are and who you want to become, somebody else is going to define that for you, especially when starting a new job.

I've created an essential exercise that will help you form what I call your *Interview Constellation*—a working and evolving guide you can use to anchor you throughout your interview journey.

Interview Constellation Exercise

What are the three reasons YOU want this job?

1. _____
_____
2. _____
_____
3. _____
_____

Note the emphasis on *you*—why YOU want this job. Not why your spouse, or your parents, or whoever else wants this for you.

Once you answer these, I encourage you to answer the following as well.

If you get this job . . .

- **#1.** What's the positive impact you want it to have on your life?
- **#2.** How do you want to feel going to that job every day?
- **#3.** How much money do you want to make?
- **#4.** What benefits and perks do you want (health, dental, and vision insurance; retirement support such as a 401(k) with a 5 percent match; flexible work-from-home policy; four-day workweek; paid time off, vacation; stipends; continuing education, support, and leadership development)?

If you can focus on who you are, why you want it, and what you want out of it, you can release a lot of pressure from others. And I promise you that you'll perform a whole lot better in your interview.

And then, if it doesn't go your way, you can be thankful. It wasn't the right fit. You know who you are, why you're doing it, and what you want. You're okay with not taking a job that you know is not for you.

Use your responses to these questions to form your *Interview Constellation*, the working and evolving guide you can use to anchor you throughout your interview journey. As when viewing a constellation in the sky, you can see how each response connects the dots into a visual representation of you.

Once you've created your *Interview Constellation*, apply it to the following universal principles for interviewing.

Universal Principles for Interviewing
Prepare

Prepare in the way that's authentic to who you are. If you don't prepare in the way that's authentic to you, you will slaughter that interview in an awkwardly bad way. You might be the "wing it" type. If that's who you are, I encourage you to wing it. If you're a little more conscientious and the thought of winging it freaks you out, then I suggest the following to help you prepare for your job interview:

- **Know yourself.** Be clear on your key skills, achievements, and value you bring to the role.
- **Know your résumé.** Be ready to discuss every detail, especially any gaps or transitions in your career.
- **Know the company.** Research their products, services, vision, mission, values, and recent news.
- **Know the job role.** Study the job description and connect your skills to the specific requirements.

- **Know the culture.** Use social media, reviews, and their website to understand their workplace environment.
- **Know the dress code.** If you're unsure, it's okay to ask the recruiter or the hiring manager what the dress code is. The common dress codes are business formal, business professional, business casual, smart casual, or casual. Dress one level above that.
- **Know how to respond to common questions.** Tell me about yourself. Why should we hire you?

Be on Time

Show up on time. Obviously.

If it's remote, confirm what the meeting software is. Download it. Make sure you understand it and that your audio is clear and you can clearly hear them. Make sure your lighting is good. Enter into the digital call five minutes before.

If it's in person, how far's the drive? Is there traffic? Construction? What if you get a flat tire? Where are you going to park? How far into the building do you have to go? You can be outside the building whenever you want, but don't be an hour before your interview in the waiting room. Plan to be in the waiting room fifteen minutes before.

Be Authentic

It's sad, but people lie in their résumés all the time. They also lie in interviews. I don't always know for sure when this is happening, but I usually *feel* it's happening. Especially if you're lying about your level of interest in the job (which might also mean you're lying to yourself).

Regardless of whether the interviewer knows you're lying, *the bill comes due at some point*. So either you pay the price now, by being honest with yourself and interviewing on your skills, achievements, value you bring to the role, and actual interest, or you get the job and you pay the price later, because deception tends to unravel with time. Just skip this step entirely.

Instead, be authentic, showcase your genuine self, and try to align your responses with the needs of the role.

- **Be authentic.** Present your skills, experience, and personality without lying or masking aspects that could be perceived as weaknesses.
- **Listen.** Actively listen and provide thoughtful answers that reflect your real thoughts and motivations. Avoid rehearsed or overly generic responses.
- **Share stories.** Provide examples of challenges or mistakes and relate how you learned from them to demonstrate your resilience and growth mindset.
- **Show enthusiasm.** Let your enthusiasm and excitement for the role and the company shine through.

If you follow these four bullets, you'll build trust with the interviewer. That trust will translate into likability.

Zig Ziglar said that "people hire people they like." Hundreds of coaching clients and even my own career have only confirmed this.

Ask Questions

Remember that interviews are a two-way street. It's not just them interviewing you to make sure you're right for the job. It's your opportunity to interview them to make sure it's a company with a culture and the kind of people you want to work with. Oftentimes the interviewer is so focused on their process and getting the information they need from you that they leave only five or so minutes for your questions. Meaning you run out of time for you. So, again, lean into who you are, why you want the job, and what you want out of it by being curious, engaged, and asking questions throughout.

Think of it this way: You meet someone new and ask them a few questions to get to know them. Wouldn't it feel weird—like they aren't curious about who you are, or interested in you—if they didn't ask a single question? Asking questions is a fantastic way to build rapport and show you care.

At the very beginning, set the stage with this simple opener: "Katrina, thank you very much for making time to talk to me. How's your morning been?"

Don't overdo it but continue to ask questions to gather information, and then, from the new information, you can ask more questions. It's a repetitive yet very useful cycle.

Here are a few other questions you could ask.

What does a successful hire look like in this role?

This question takes it away from "Do you fit?" to you learning what success looks like to the company. You can then assess whether you can, or even want to, deliver said "success." It also puts them on the spot as to whether they've defined that, because a lot of times they haven't defined what a successful hire looks like.

The cousin, or equivalent, question to ask is this:

Why is this position open? Is this a new role? Is it a backfill?

No matter how they answer this question, you'll learn about the role, culture, and overall health of the company. Honestly, if the role has been open for eight months, that's a red flag. Or they might say, "We had someone go on leave and they didn't come back." This response isn't always a red flag, but I hope it prompts you to ask further questions.

If it's a new role, they might say, "We're growing quickly. We're adding one hundred new people . . ." Or they might not share that. So the natural follow-up question is, "Oh, that's amazing. What's the reason for the new role?"

If it's a backfill, then that leads to a line of questioning: "How long has the role been open? Was this an unusual situation, or has this been a difficult role to keep filled?" Pay close attention to how they answer that question, because it will give you an indicator about the job itself, the hiring manager, and the culture. This will also lead naturally to culture-based questions.

Understanding the company's motivations can help determine the list of questions you ask.

Tell me more about the team culture. What is it like?
This is a really good question. You might get a broad answer, or even a specific one. Regardless, you're going to find out a lot here. You'll probably hear about the size of the team, how they work, the hierarchy, and who influences everybody else. You could then follow up with, "What are they looking for in a leader?" or, "What are they looking for in a colleague?" This will depend on the role you're interviewing for.

The following is another framing of this question:

I'm excited about earning the opportunity to speak to the hiring manager. What are they like?
You're trying to learn more about who they are and what's important to them. If you get an answer that indicates that they are results oriented, chances are that they have a dominant workplace

behavioral style. You could then assume that you will likely be working for somebody who is a tough cookie.

If you hear that they're one of the most beloved leaders, that everyone loves them, then you'll have that to help inform your decision.

Ask questions relating to your *Interview Constellation.*
Ask open-ended questions to see whether the role is going to fit the criteria you have for happiness. For example, if there's a requirement to be in the office every single day, and it's a one-hour commute, that means your work week actually entails fifty hours. Is that okay with you? Maybe they give a car stipend or allowance. Inquire. You need to consider the total energy commitment on your life. What time will you need to wake up? How often will you see your kids? Making $50,000 less a year to be at every one of your daughter's dance recitals might be worth it to you. Or you might be okay with the drive and time away from home, but consider everything.

You might love the job so much that the cons aren't that big of a deal. Remember the *authentic* piece, and don't lie to yourself. If the impact is the impact you want on your life, go for it.

Answering Questions

One of the most popular frameworks to answer behavioral questions is the STAR method. (Example: Tell me about a time that you were in a difficult situation with a colleague or boss. Tell me what it was and how you approached it.) But I'm not a big fan of it.

It's not real. It's not based on real-life work experiences. It also doesn't give you the opportunity to provide the information that they *need*.

In regard to a framework for answering questions, it boils down to these three things:

1. **If you're informed at any point to answer in a certain way (STAR, for example), do it.** One core reason is compliance. It helps them build the same rules to measure everybody by. Another reason is they want to know whether you can follow instructions.
2. **If you are not given guidance on a particular type of interviewing methodology, then be yourself, be authentic, be conversational, and be professional.** When someone asks you a question, answer knowing where you want to land. Get down to the root. Lean toward evidence and provide examples. Stories help. Focus your answers around solving problems, providing outcomes, and delivering results. What was the problem you were up against? What were the things that you did to help solve the problem? What was the outcome?
3. **Read the room with every single interviewer.** Some people have a more conversational body language. Pick up on what you can. Body language sets tone. Open? Guarded? If the interviewer is guarded, and you're responding openly, that creates a bit of awkward polarity. Now don't take this to contradict everything I've said about authenticity, but meet them where they are. Don't reflect and mirror them, but respect the body language, verbal cues, and tone of voice. Match it in your own authentic way.

Time Check

If you're in an interview, it's usually a good sign if you go over time with them. Let them drive thought. But I do recommend saying something like, "Hey, I just want to check in with you. I'm so loving our conversation. I know we're supposed to wrap in nine minutes. I can go over if you can. But I wanted to check in." This will demonstrate your mindfulness of time management, and it will subliminally reaffirm your interest. Win-win. They might say, "Oh my, thank you so much. I'm really loving talking to you. I can go over if you can, no problem." Keep going.

If an interview wraps up early, it's not always negative. It usually means they have exactly what they need. They'll usually provide some context: "I've got what I need and want to move forward with you."

Wrapping Things Up

You've got to read the room and be true to your approach. Feel it out. In general, wrap up with something like this: "I've really enjoyed our conversation and would love the opportunity to keep the conversation going. Is there anything you need from me? Any questions or concerns that I can address?"

They might say, for example, "My only concern is you don't have this degree/certification." This gives you an opportunity to address the concern. Don't respond in a defensive way. Instead, try to instill a bit more confidence.

The way they answer your parting question is going to tell you their level of interest in you. They might ask you to schedule later in the week. But don't stress if they don't. They have a lot to process. They have to decide whether they want to move to the next step with you. So don't ruin a great interview by being too pushy on the next steps.

But it's totally reasonable to ask, "What are the next steps?" or, "When are you looking to make a decision?"

Follow Up

- **#1.** Send a thank-you note right after the interview.
- **#2.** Check in again a week after the interview.
- **#3.** Check in two weeks after the interview.
- **#4.** Check in four weeks after the interview.

Life might intervene, especially if you're working and you're interviewing, but make sure that you send a thank-you note (#1) before the end of the day. And in the worst-case scenario, send it within twenty-four hours. You can write something like, "Hey, I just wanted to send you a quick note thanking you for your time today. I really enjoyed our chat. I'm even more excited about the role. [Call out one thing that they mentioned that was important to them.] If there's anything else that you need from me, let me know. I hope you have a wonderful day."

No one's going to get mad at you for following up once a week for two weeks. So send another one a week later (#2). Write something like, "Hey, I'm checking in and am curious if you have a timeline for your decision, or if you want me to sit tight and wait to hear from you. Thanks, and I hope you're having a good week."

Now, if you're two weeks out from the interview, and you've sent two follow-ups and haven't heard anything, You might be thinking, *I haven't heard anything. They don't like me. What's going on?*

They might be thinking the following: *You're still being considered, but the head count's on hold, or so-and-so is having a baby, so it's slowing down the process.* Things may be happening that you don't know about and that have nothing to do with you. If it does have to do with you, consider yourself lucky.

Then send out another one (#3): "I hope you're having a great week! Just wanted to check if there's any update on the timeline for the [position name] decision. Let me know if there's anything else you need from me."

Give it another two weeks and then send another (#4). This time, give them an out so you're not pestering them, but you're looking for a sign of whether they want to move forward: "Hey, checking in. I'm here whenever you know you're ready to move forward. I am actively interviewing and have a couple of things that have progressed. I appreciate the opportunity for this role, and unless I hear something different from you, I will be pursuing those other opportunities."

In other words, you have four to five weeks. If the recruiter or the hiring manager hasn't gotten back to you in that time, it's a red flag.

Video Follow-Up?

If somebody's Gen Z or a millennial, and you text over a video follow-up, that will probably land well. But you don't know the demographic of the ultimate decision-maker, and you don't know whether somebody is old-school. So if you send them a text with a video, or an email, recruiters can be a bit petty sometimes (sadly): *I can't believe that dude sent me that video.* And you could 100 percent disqualify yourself. Right then and there. Or they might have this response: *Oh my, I love him so much. He just sent me a quick video? That's amazing.* But it's risky, so tread lightly. Read the room!

Focus on the Long Game

I recently had a coaching session with a person who said something profound. I said, "Okay, say that back to me again." And they said, "What? I don't know what I said. I feel all over the place." And I said, "Your tone changed and your shoulders went down when I heard you say, 'I just want to work somewhere when I can show up every day and just be myself.'" And they said, "I said that?" And then they paused and said, "Yeah, that really is it."

If you show up as yourself and you don't get the job, it's not the end of the world. You dodged a bullet. Count it as practice and repetition. Count it as a blessing because you don't have to show up to a job and hide. Just like this person, you deserve to work somewhere where you can show up every day and just be yourself.

Regardless of how the interview goes and what's happening with your follow-up, keep at your job search. Don't stop! Your next career move isn't real until two things happen: (1) you get an offer and (2) you accept the offer.

If you get the offer (yes!), but don't say yes right away; there's a lot to consider. And with that, I'll pass it back to Craig to help you seal the deal!

—*Erika*
Connect with me on:
- *LinkedIn: https://www.linkedin.com/in/eoliver*
- *And check out my website: newton-haus.com*

KEY TAKEAWAYS

- **Know yourself.** Reflect on who you are and why you want the job. Use the *Interview Constellation Exercise* to clarify your motivations, desired impact, and goals.
- **Prepare authentically.** Tailor your preparation style to what works for you. Research the company, role, and culture, and be ready to discuss your skills, achievements, and résumé details.

- **Be punctual and polished.** Show up on time, prepare for potential delays, and ensure your virtual or in-person setup is professional.
- **Be authentic.** Present yourself truthfully, showcase your real skills and experiences, and build rapport with honesty and enthusiasm.
- **Ask thoughtful questions.** Engage with the interviewer by asking meaningful questions about the role, team culture, and expectations, aligning them with your personal goals and values.
- **Follow up professionally.** Send a thank-you note within twenty-four hours, follow up weekly if needed, and be respectful of their process. Adjust your tone and frequency based on their responsiveness.
- **Play the long game.** If it's not the right fit, view the experience as practice. Aim to find a role where you can show up authentically and thrive.
- **When you get the offer, don't say yes right away.** Take all the time you need to ensure that the job is a good fit.

CHAPTER 11:

Seal the Deal

(Start Strong)

Congratulations! You've made it through the application process, interviews, and follow-ups, and now you're staring at that long-awaited job offer.

This moment feels like a big win ... because it is. But before you pop the champagne, there are still a few steps to navigate. This chapter is your guide to sealing the deal and starting strong.

Receiving the Offer: First Things First

The job offer typically comes in one of two ways: a phone call or an email. If it's a call, listen carefully and express gratitude. Resist the urge to accept on the spot—even if you're excited. Thank them for the offer, ask for details in writing, and let them know you'll take some time to review it. Employers expect this, so don't feel pressured to commit immediately.

Once you receive the written offer, dive into the details. Look beyond the salary. Review the benefits package, bonuses, vacation days, and other perks. Are there hidden gems like a 401(k) match, tuition reimbursement, or remote work flexibility? These can add tremendous value to the overall compensation.

Negotiating with Confidence

If you're nervous about negotiating, you're not alone. But here's the thing: Most companies expect you to negotiate. The key is to approach it with confidence and professionalism.

1. **Do your homework.** Research your market value. Sites like Glassdoor, PayScale, and LinkedIn Salary can give you insights into what similar roles in your area pay. If you have industry contacts, don't hesitate to ask them about typical salaries for the area. Knowledge is power, and walking into a negotiation with data makes you more credible.
2. **Anchor on value, not desire.** When negotiating, focus on the value you bring to the company rather than just what you want. For example: "Given my experience in [specific skill], I'd love to see the salary closer to $85,000" is much stronger than "I'd like $85,000 because I think I deserve it."
3. **Consider the whole package.** If the salary isn't flexible, look at other areas. Can you negotiate additional vacation days, remote work options, or a signing bonus? Some companies are more willing to adjust these than base pay.
4. **Practice your delivery.** Negotiations are a conversation, not a battle. Be polite, professional, and collaborative. A phrase like "I'm excited about the opportunity and want to make sure we find a package that works for both of us" sets the right tone.

Accepting the Offer: Closing the Deal

Once you've agreed on terms, it's time to accept the offer formally.

This is often done via email, though some companies may send a digital form to sign. Here's a simple response:

"Thank you for the opportunity to join [Company Name] as [Position]. I'm excited to contribute to your team and am grateful for the support during this process. I officially accept the offer and look forward to my start date on [Date]. Please let me know if there's anything else you need from me in the meantime."

Before you hit send, confirm any final details like start dates, onboarding instructions, and expectations for your first day.

Starting Your New Job: Day One and Beyond

The first ninety days in your new role are critical. They set the tone for how you're perceived and establish your foundation for long-term success.

1. **Prepare for onboarding.** Whether it's in person or virtual, make sure you know what's expected on day one. Ask for a copy of the onboarding schedule in advance and check that you have all necessary equipment, log-ins, or training materials.
2. **Make a strong first impression.** Show up on time (early is better), dress appropriately, and bring a positive attitude. Be curious, respectful, and eager to learn. Take notes during meetings, introduce yourself to colleagues, and ask thoughtful questions.
3. **Build relationships.** Your technical skills got you the job, but relationships will help you thrive. Take time to get to know your team and other stakeholders. Who are the decision-makers? Who are the influencers? Build rapport by being approachable and reliable.
4. **Clarify expectations.** Sit down with your manager early

on to discuss goals, priorities, and how success will be measured in your role. This shows initiative and ensures you're aligned from the start.

5. **Be patient with yourself.** Starting a new job can feel overwhelming, and that's okay. Give yourself grace as you learn the ropes. Focus on progress, not perfection, and don't be afraid to ask for help when you need it.

6. **Document every great outcome.** Maintain a Google Doc to capture your accomplishments, accompanied by outcomes and screenshots of positive feedback or recognition. Leverage this for reviews and opportunities—evidence of your value. Always be prepared to showcase your contributions.

7. **As always . . . keep painting your store.** Don't close that LLC of yours. Stay open and flexible to any and all opportunities. Update your LinkedIn profile. Stay active and participate on LinkedIn. Maintain an engaging and professional online presence. Remember, your career is defined by the personal brand you build, not by a single employer or job title. Treat your career as a portfolio of achievements under a unique identity that reflects your expertise and journey.

Receiving a job offer is exciting, but it's just the beginning of your next chapter. By evaluating your offer carefully, negotiating with confidence, and starting your new role with intention, you set yourself up for long-term success. Remember, this is your store! Own it, and make it one you're proud of.

You've got this!

KEY TAKEAWAYS

- **Evaluate the offer thoughtfully.** Express gratitude but avoid accepting immediately. Request the offer in writing and review the full package—salary, benefits, perks, and growth opportunities.
- **Negotiate with confidence.** Research market value to support your case. Focus on the value you bring, not just your desires. Negotiate beyond salary, considering bonuses, flexibility, or vacation days. Approach conversations politely and collaboratively.
- **Accept the offer.** Confirm your acceptance in writing. Clarify start dates, onboarding, and any remaining details before signing.
- **Start strong in your new role.** Prepare for onboarding by understanding expectations and gathering necessary materials. Make a positive impression with punctuality, professionalism, and curiosity. Build relationships by connecting with colleagues and understanding team dynamics. Align with your manager early on to clarify goals and success metrics.
- **Track your accomplishments from day one to showcase your value later.** You should always be prepared to show off your contributions!
- **Keep painting your store.** Consistency over time is key. Too many people abandon their content and engagement strategy when they land a new job and don't resurface until they need to network for their next job. It's much better to keep your audience warm. Keep your LinkedIn and professional presence active, treating your career as a portfolio of achievements that reflects your unique expertise and journey.

CONCLUSION:

Be Human

(Always)

Painting your store is more than just a metaphor—it's your road map to career success. It's about crafting a vibrant display that tells the world who you are, what you offer, and why they should step inside. Like a great storefront, your personal brand must be inviting, memorable, and unmistakably you. Whether you're job hunting, advancing in your career, or building your own thing, how you "paint" your store determines the opportunities and connections you attract.

Here's the truth: Painting your store isn't about a quick touch-up for a one-time impression—it's about creating something lasting. It's about showing up in the world as visible, valuable, and authentic in ways that stand out. In a landscape dominated by algorithms and automation, the human touch remains your greatest competitive advantage.

The job market isn't a straight path; it's a living, shifting ecosystem. Opportunities come from the relationships we nurture, the value we deliver, and the unique ways we choose to show up.

Your personal brand isn't a polished highlight reel of your greatest hits. It's your story—an ever-evolving mix of experiences, values, and aspirations that make you relatable, trustworthy, and, most important, memorable. When you embrace this mindset, you're not just preparing for your next job—you're creating a legacy.

As you move forward, take these final thoughts with you:

1. **Be the SME of you.** No one knows your story better than you do. Own it, share it boldly, and let the world see what makes you remarkable.
2. **Keep painting.** Your personal brand isn't static. It grows, adapts, and reflects the best of who you are becoming.
3. **Take the leap.** In life, sometimes you just have to jump and learn as you go.
4. **Give before you ask.** Whether in life or on LinkedIn, the 5:1 give-to-ask ratio isn't just good strategy—it's how you build trust and foster meaningful connections.
5. **As always, stay human.** Empathy and authenticity aren't just buzzwords—they're your edge in a world that often forgets to put people first.

Thank you for letting me be part of your journey.
Now it's your chance to paint something that's uniquely yours.
Go forward with courage, creativity, and confidence.
The world is waiting.

HOW I'LL APPLY THIS

HEADS UP!

Beware of Job Scams

(Navigating the Hidden Dangers of the Job Search)

In today's digital world, job hunting has become more convenient—but also more dangerous. As job seekers, we're conditioned to trust that the platforms we apply through are secure, that the jobs we find are legitimate, and that our information is protected. Unfortunately, that's not always the case. Scammers have gotten smarter, more organized, and increasingly bold. And it's not just individuals who are vulnerable—employers are facing risks too.

We live in an era where anyone can create a fake job posting, duplicate a company's website, or mimic a legitimate recruiter's voice online. And if you're not vigilant, it's easy to fall into their traps. Scammers are preying on our desperation, our urgency to find work, and our belief that the online job world is trustworthy. But I'm here to tell you—it's not all doom and gloom. With the right awareness and strategies, you can protect yourself from job scams and navigate your job search safely.

The Rise of Job Scams

During a recent podcast with my friend Mark Anthony Dyson, host of *The Voice of Job Seekers*,[7] we dove deep into the growing threat of job scams. We've both seen firsthand how scammers are taking advantage of job seekers, and we've experienced it ourselves. Whether you're a traditional worker or a freelancer, the risk is real, and the tactics are evolving.

Scammers often replicate legitimate job postings, creating entire fake websites or profiles on platforms like LinkedIn. Their goal? To collect your personal information, steal your identity, or trick you into paying for services that will "guarantee" you a job. One of the most alarming trends we discussed is how these scammers are even impersonating recruiters for well-known companies, making it incredibly difficult to differentiate between real and fake opportunities.

In fact, there are even reports of scammers using your identity to get hired themselves! According to an article on CNET, identity thieves are going so far as to use real job seekers' information—like names, Social Security numbers, and even résumés—to get hired for remote jobs.[8] Once they're in, they use their access to commit fraud, leaving the real job seeker completely unaware until it's too late.

How to Spot a Job Scam

So how can you protect yourself? Here are some key red flags to watch out for:

---

7 Mark Anthony Dyson, "Had Enough of Job Scams? Here's How To Protect Yourself.," Youtube @MarkAnthonyDyson, July 30, 2024, accessed February 24, 2025, 29:12, https://www.youtube.com/watch?v=mCVemosfFMc.

8 Holly Johnson, "It's Not a Real Job. It's an Employment Scam," CNET, January 14, 2025, accessed February 24, 2025, https://www.cnet.com/personal-finance/its-not-a-real-job-its-an-employment-scam/.

1. **Unusual communication.** If you receive an unsolicited email or message offering you a job, be wary. Legitimate employers rarely contact candidates out of the blue without prior interaction. If a recruiter or company representative reaches out to you without any context, double-check their credentials and verify their identity.
2. **Vague job descriptions.** Scammers often post vague or too-good-to-be-true job listings. If the job description doesn't specify clear responsibilities, qualifications, or expectations, take a step back. Real job listings are detailed and explain exactly what the company is looking for.
3. **Requests for personal information too soon.** A common tactic is to ask for personal information early in the process, including your Social Security number, bank details, or even a scan of your driver's license. Legitimate employers don't need this information until much later in the hiring process, typically after an offer has been made.
4. **Pressure to act quickly.** If you're feeling rushed to apply, send information, or pay for a service related to the job, it's likely a scam. Scammers rely on creating a sense of urgency to prevent you from doing your due diligence.
5. **Unprofessional communication.** If the email contains poor grammar, strange formatting, or an unusual sender address (for example, a Gmail address rather than a company domain), it's worth investigating further.
6. **Payment for application.** Never, under any circumstances, should you have to pay to apply for a job or get hired. If a company asks you to pay for training, certifications, or special placement, it's a scam.

Protecting Yourself from Identity Theft in the Job Search

As CNET's article points out, identity thieves are increasingly sophisticated, using your personal information to commit fraud.[9] If your identity is stolen, it can take years to repair the damage. Here's how to protect yourself:

1. **Limit the information you share.** Be cautious about what you include on your résumé. Your full address, Social Security number, and even your complete date of birth are not necessary. Stick to the essentials: your name, email, phone number, and location (city and state).
2. **Verify the company and recruiter.** If you're applying to a job through a job board, always cross-check the company's website. Does the job exist on their official careers page? If a recruiter contacts you, look them up on LinkedIn. Make sure their profile is legitimate, and reach out to the company directly if you have doubts.
3. **Use secure platforms.** Stick to well-known and secure job boards and platforms. Scammers often create fake websites that mimic legitimate job boards, but reputable platforms have security measures in place to protect you.
4. **Monitor your credit.** Regularly check your credit report to ensure no one is opening accounts in your name. If you notice anything suspicious, take action immediately by freezing your credit.

What Employers Are Doing

It's not just job seekers who are feeling the effects of job scams—employers are grappling with the fallout too. Scammers are

---

9 Holly Johnson, "It's Not a Real Job. It's an Employment Scam," CNET, January 14, 2025, accessed February 24, 2025, https://www.cnet.com/personal-finance/its-not-a-real-job-its-an-employment-scam/.

scraping legitimate job postings from ATSs, reposting them on fake job boards, and charging applicants to apply. They're also impersonating recruiters, tarnishing the reputations of real companies.

In response, many employers are adding "What to Expect" sections to their careers pages, offering transparency about their hiring processes to help candidates recognize legitimate interactions. Companies like Nvidia, for example, have detailed pages outlining their interview process so that job seekers can compare any communication they receive against the official process.

As a job seeker, if you ever have doubts, check the company's website for these kinds of details. And remember, if a job posting looks suspicious, it probably is. Take the extra step to verify its legitimacy—better to be safe than sorry.

The Importance of Being Vigilant

Scammers are smart, but so are you. By staying informed and vigilant, you can protect yourself from falling victim to job scams. Always do your research, trust your instincts, and don't rush into any job that doesn't feel right.

As we discussed on the podcast, scammers rely on our behavior—our tendency to apply to jobs en masse without vetting every listing, and our assumption that every job offer is legitimate. But we need to approach the job search with more care. Double-check every opportunity, speak to real people, and always look for warning signs.

With the rise of job scams, it's more important than ever to approach your job search strategically. Build real relationships, verify information, and trust your gut. If something feels off, step back and investigate. It's your career—and your identity—on the line. Stay safe.

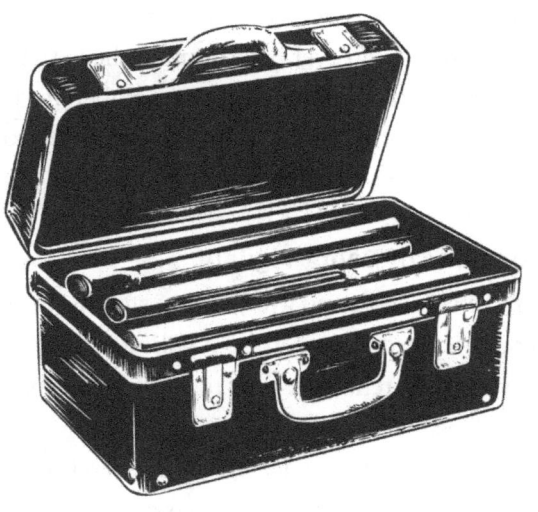

BONUS

Tools & Tech

(Take a Few Things With You)

Optimizing Your Job Search with Teal HQ

In today's fast-paced and competitive job market, leveraging technology can be a game changer for job seekers. Tools like TealHQ provide an invaluable resource to help you build better résumés, tailor them to specific job descriptions, and track your application progress. But as useful as these tools are, it's critical to remember they are just that—tools. Success in your job search requires strategy, critical thinking, and, yes, a personal touch. Let's dive into how you can use TealHQ effectively without losing sight of what makes you unique.

Writing Better Résumés with TealHQ

TealHQ offers a user-friendly platform for crafting résumés that stand out. One of its best features is the ability to upload your existing résumé and have it analyzed for strengths and weaknesses. The tool provides tips on improving formatting, highlighting accomplishments, and using action-oriented language.

While this is a fantastic starting point, don't let the tool do all the work. Automation is great at identifying gaps, but it can't tell the nuanced story of your career. Your résumé should showcase not just what you've done but how you've added value. Think of it this way: AI might find the keywords, but only you can tell the story.

Pro Tip: Use TealHQ's insights as a guide, but spend time crafting a summary that communicates your professional journey in a way that resonates with your target audience. Include specific achievements and metrics whenever possible, but also weave in elements of your personality and unique skill set.

Job Matching and Résumé Tailoring

One of TealHQ's standout features is its job-matching functionality. By uploading a job description, you can compare it to your résumé and see where you align—and where you don't. The tool suggests keywords and phrases you can incorporate into your résumé to increase the likelihood of passing ATSs.

However, don't simply copy and paste those suggestions into your résumé without reflection. Employers aren't just looking for someone who checks the right boxes—they want someone who demonstrates initiative, creativity, and authenticity.

Here's how to get the most out of this feature:

1. **Understand the keywords.** TealHQ might flag terms like "project management" or "budget forecasting," but it's up to you to embed those keywords naturally into your accomplishments. Instead of simply stating "Experienced in project management," try "Led a $2M project from initiation to completion, delivering results 10% under budget."
2. **Personalize every time.** Tailoring doesn't mean rewriting your résumé from scratch for every application. Instead,

tweak the sections that matter most—your professional summary, core skills, and key achievements.

Tracking Your Applications

Organization is key when you're applying for multiple jobs. TealHQ provides a tracker that enables you to log the details of each application—company name, job title, submission date, and follow-up actions. This feature ensures you never miss a deadline or forget where you stand in the process.

But remember that tracking isn't just about logistics; it's also an opportunity to reflect. Regularly review your progress. Are you getting callbacks? If not, is it because your applications are too generic? Use the tracker as a feedback loop to refine your approach.

You're the Captain, Tools Are the Copilots

Think of TealHQ as your copilot, not the captain of your job search. It can save time and boost efficiency, but it's not a replacement for you. The context matters—AI might suggest inserting buzzwords, but without proper context, they can make your résumé feel robotic. Your voice and narrative must remain central.

Podcasts

Podcasts have emerged as a powerful and portable way to learn, explore, and grow. Whether you're a job seeker, entrepreneur, or lifelong learner, platforms like Spotify, Apple Podcasts, and Google Podcasts are treasure troves of knowledge. When used strategically, podcasts can become your secret weapon for research, inspiration, and personal development.

Unlike books or articles, they offer the unique benefit of hearing directly from thought leaders, industry insiders, and innovators in a conversational format. The voices behind the mic often share candid stories, behind-the-scenes tips, and nuanced perspectives you won't find elsewhere.

Finding the Right Podcasts

Finding the right podcasts for you can feel overwhelming. The following are a few tips to curate a playlist that works for you:

1. **Search.** Use podcast platforms like Spotify, Apple Podcasts, and Google Podcasts to search for keywords related to your field or topic of interest. For example, type in "marketing trends," "job search tips," or "leadership lessons" to discover relevant shows.
2. **Get recommendations from friends, colleagues, or others in your industry.** Ask: "What podcasts do you like?"
3. **Look for credibility.** Check the podcast host's background and guest lineup. Are they reputable in their field? Check reviews and ratings.
4. **Follow diverse perspectives.** Don't limit yourself to a single genre or viewpoint. Some of the best ideas come from cross-disciplinary learning.

Using Podcasts for Career Growth and Networking

Podcasts aren't just about info; they can be a gateway to career opportunities and professional relationships too.

- **Identify industry trends.** Podcasts often discuss the latest innovations and shifts in the market. By tuning into thought leaders, you can anticipate where your field is headed and position yourself as a forward-thinking candidate or professional.

- **Learn the language.** Listening to experts in your industry helps you pick up jargon, frameworks, and cultural references that can enhance your conversations in interviews or networking events.
- **Engage with hosts and guests.** Most podcast hosts and guests have active LinkedIn profiles or social media accounts. If you hear something that resonates, don't hesitate to reach out. Send a thoughtful message about how their episode impacted you—it's a great way to start a genuine conversation.
- **Spot hidden opportunities.** Guests on podcasts often discuss challenges they're facing. This can give you a heads-up on potential needs in their company or industry. Use this insight to craft solutions or ideas that set you apart.

Final Thought

Use a note-taking app to jot down takeaways, quotes, or action items. Save your favorite ones and curate playlists.

Tools to Paint Your Store with Engaging Content
Camtasia

Camtasia is my go-to for editing polished videos. It's intuitive and powerful, allowing you to cut, splice, and enhance your footage with ease. Use it to create tutorial-style videos, screen recordings, or product walk-throughs. Camtasia also includes features for adding transitions, callouts, and overlays that give your content a professional edge.

Pro Tip: Use Camtasia's annotation tools to highlight key points in your video, making your message crystal clear.

iPhone

For quick, high-quality content, nothing beats the simplicity of your iPhone. The camera is excellent, and with apps like iMovie or by directly syncing to editing platforms, you can create sharp, professional-looking videos in minutes. Bonus: Your phone is always with you, so you can capture ideas and moments as they happen.

Pro Tip: Invest in a small tripod or gimbal for smoother, steadier videos, and shoot in well-lit areas for the best results.

Opus Pro

This AI-driven platform is a game changer for enhancing your content's impact. Opus Pro allows you to create standout videos with dynamic visuals, captions, and effects. It even uses AI to help you optimize your content for social media algorithms, ensuring it performs well across platforms.

Pro Tip: Use Opus Pro's tools to auto-generate captions, which improve accessibility and engagement.

Streamyard

Streamyard makes live streaming easy and professional. Whether you're hosting a webinar, leading a panel, or giving a thought-leadership talk, this platform ensures seamless broadcasting. It also allows you to stream to multiple platforms simultaneously—like LinkedIn Live, YouTube, and Facebook.

Pro Tip: Use Streamyard's branding features to add your logo, overlays, and a call-to-action banner, reinforcing your SME status.

HOW I'LL APPLY THIS

About the Author

Craig Fisher is a renowned speaker, author, and consultant who has dedicated his career to helping individuals and organizations navigate the evolving world of work. With over two decades of experience in talent acquisition, employer branding, and career development, Craig has become a trusted voice for job seekers and employers alike. Known for his engaging style and practical advice, he brings a human touch to an increasingly automated job market.

Craig's journey into recruiting began in an unconventional way. Armed with a background in advertising and an entrepreneurial spirit, he quickly found himself drawn to the world of technology staffing and recruitment. Over the years, Craig honed his expertise by blending creative marketing strategies with deep insights into the hiring process, becoming a pioneer in leveraging tools like LinkedIn, social media, and content marketing to connect talent with opportunity.

He's the founder of TalentNet Media, a consulting and training firm that has worked with some of the world's most iconic brands, helping them attract, engage, and retain top talent. His work has also been featured at conferences, webinars, and in publications across the globe. Craig is the creator of the popular TalentNet Live events, where thought leaders, recruiters, and HR professionals gather to share innovative strategies and foster meaningful connections.

Craig's first book, *Hiring Humans*, delves into the balance of technology and empathy in the recruiting process, advocating for the importance of building authentic relationships in a tech-driven world. His latest work, *Paint Your Store*, builds on this foundation, empowering readers to craft their personal brands, position themselves as subject matter experts, and take control of their careers.

Beyond his professional accomplishments, Craig is a self-proclaimed technology nerd, a lover of storytelling, and a champion of kindness in the workplace. When he's not writing or speaking, you'll find him spending time with his family, hiking around Grapevine Lake, or shamelessly using his three sons as examples in his presentations.

Craig's philosophy is simple: Every person has a unique story to tell and a talent to offer. His mission is to help others discover their strengths, share their stories, and thrive in their professional journeys. Because at the end of the day, Craig believes that hiring isn't just about filling roles—it's about connecting humans with opportunities that help them flourish.

KEY TAKEAWAYS

- 🌐 talentnetlive.com | fishdogs.com
- in linkedin.com/in/wcraigfisher/
- @fishdogs
- ▶ Craig Fisher
- f @TalentNetEvents

www.ingramcontent.com/pod-product-compliance
Lightning Source LLC
Chambersburg PA
CBHW060503030426
42337CB00015B/1709